KAZAKHSTAN DEVELOPMENT FINANCE ASSESSMENT

FEBRUARY 2021

ADB

ASIAN DEVELOPMENT BANK

ISBN 978-92-9262-654-9 (print);978-92-9262-655-6 (electronic); 978-92-9262-656-3 (ebook)
Publication Stock No. TCS200428-2
DOI: http://dx.doi.org/10.22617/TCS200428-2

Commissioned by the Asian Development Bank (ADB) and UNDP. Drafted by Gregory De Paepe, independent consultant, and TALAP Center for Applied Research, under the supervision of Aigerim Yegemberdiyeva (United Nations Development Programme) and Genadiy Rau (ADB).

Preliminary findings of this analysis were presented at the First "Regional SDG Summit: Mobilization of financial resources for the implementation of sustainable development goals" organized by the Government of Kazakhstan with the support of ADB and the United Nations Development Programme in Kazakhstan, that took place on 15-16 November 2019.

Contents

Tables, Figures, and Boxes

Boxes

Foreword

Meeting the United Nation's 2030 Agenda requires unprecedented investment from different sources of finance, ambitious strategies, and structural reform. A challenge for governments around the world is to ensure that resources are raised, channeled, and translated into measurable results to meet the targets set by the Sustainable Development Goals (SDGs). Coupled with the volatile macroeconomic, financial and political environment, the capacity of governments to mobilize, sequence, and make effective use of financing sources is more than ever at the center of the SDGs' debate.

With the aim of responding to the growing demand of countries which are not seeking only larger, but also better quality SDG financing, the United Nations Development Programme (UNDP) has developed the Development Finance Assessment (DFA)—a range of tools in support of these efforts that offers a comprehensive analysis of existing financial resources and identifies opportunities to strengthen the overall institutional financing architecture.

In 2019, UNDP and the Kazakhstan Resident Mission of the Asian Development Bank (ADB) joined forces and delivered a first phase of the DFA aiming to assess the opportunities and challenges Kazakhstan is facing to mobilize the investment needed to achieve the SDGs' 2030 Agenda and its own Strategy 2050. The DFA presents a comprehensive analysis of trends in public and private finance, along with existing policies and partnerships in place. It discussed the usefulness for Kazakhstan to establish a financing mechanism to maximize development finance and inform resource allocation to achieve the SDG targets.

We hope that the practical recommendations made in this report will be used as a basis for constructive dialogue and action across public and private actors.

We look forward to continue working with all national counterparts, development partners and other stakeholders to follow-up on the findings outlined in this assessment toward accelerating SDG financing in Kazakhstan.

ADB and UNDP country teams

Abbreviations

ADB	Asian Development Bank
AIFC	Astana International Financial Center
ASEAN	Association of Southeast Asian Nations
CCA	Caucasus and Central Asia
CIF	Climate Investment Funds
CIT	corporate income tax
CPEIR	Climate Public Expenditure and Institutional Review
CPSD	country private sector diagnostic
CRS	creditor reporting system
CSR	corporate social responsibility
DFA	development finance assessment
EBRD	European Bank for Reconstruction and Development
EECCA	Eastern Europe, the Caucasus and Central Asia
EIB	European Investment Bank
ERI	Economic Research Institute
FDI	foreign direct investment
FSED	Forecast of social and economic development
GCF	Green Climate Fund
GDP	gross domestic product
GHG	greenhouse gas
IFC	International Finance Corporation
IFI	international financial institution
IFSB	Islamic Financial Services Board
INDC	Intended Nationally Determined Contribution

INFF	Integrated National Financing Framework
LIC	low-income country
MES	Ministry of Education and Science of the Republic of Kazakhstan
MNE	Ministry of National Economy of the Republic of Kazakhstan
MoF	Ministry of Finance of the Republic of Kazakhstan
MFI	microfinance institution
MTEF	medium-term expenditure framework
NBK	National Bank of Kazakhstan
NFRK	National Fund of the Republic of Kazakhstan
NGO	nongovernment organization
NPL	nonperforming loan
ODA	official development assistance
OECD	Organisation for Economic Co-operation and Development
OOF	other official flows
PFM	public financial management
PIT	personal income tax
PPP	public-private partnership
SDG	Sustainable Development Goal
SMEs	small and medium-sized enterprises
SOE	state-owned enterprise
UMIC	upper middle-income countries
UPF	Unified Pension Fund
VAT	value-added tax
VNR	voluntary national review

Executive Summary

Both the quality and quantity of Kazakhstan's development finance are under strain. Total available development finance stagnated in recent years and decreased significantly as a share of gross domestic product, from 64% in 2010 to 39% in 2018. The composition of total development finance also evolved markedly, away from a reliance on international capital inflows throughout the country's economic growth boom since its independence, toward an increasing reliance on domestic public revenue, mostly taxes.

The common, underlying driver of these structural changes in Kazakhstan's development finance landscape is the evolution of international resource prices. The end of the commodity super cycle has led to the sharp decline of largely resource-seeking foreign direct investment (FDI) inflows and undermined government revenue through its impact on oil-related taxes and export revenues. This points to the critical importance of diversifying away from a resource-fueled growth model toward an inclusive and diversified, private-sector led development model. Embarking on this overarching, long-term development finance agenda would underpin higher and more sustainable government revenue as well as more closely involving non-state, commercial actors in the financing of Kazakhstan's development priorities.

While there are no forward-looking estimates available of the total resources Kazakhstan needs either to realize its development strategy Kazakhstan-2050, nor to finance its 2030 Agenda for Sustainable Development (2030 Agenda), there are indications that the current relative amount and mix of financial resources will fall short of financing needs. Implementing the government's multiple development strategies increasingly relies mostly on public finance, following the strong decline of FDI and the persistent low domestic commercial investment. The direct negative impact of declining government revenue in recent years on social spending per capita illustrates the government's limited fiscal space to implement its national development plans.

Kazakhstan's state planning system currently does not explicitly identify and direct the scale and types of public and private financing that will be needed to deliver the investments and services required by the country's long-term development strategy. Articulating a clear long-term vision on resource needs and their strategic allocation could therefore support more stable budgeting practices and long-term fiscal sustainability.

Kazakhstan's development finance agenda therefore consists of two main sets of interrelated actions: authorities need to (i) maximize the developmental impact of their available, scarce development resources, mostly public; and (ii) undertake the necessary policy reforms to diversify increase available financial resources over the medium term. Authorities may consider the value of developing a holistic, long-term development finance strategy in line with the financing needs of its development strategy Kazakhstan-2050.

Kazakhstan's formal State Planning System provides a strong basis to guide the country's socioeconomic development over the medium- and long-term. Strategic planning is well-established throughout the government, allowing for a more strategic allocation of resources. The downside to the extensive State Planning System is the emergence of multiple, competing priorities and duplication across national and sectoral programs, which could be addressed by streamlining priorities and having a tighter focus on implementation.

As a result, the de facto implementation of Kazakhstan's State Planning System is not as advanced as its de jure institutional and regulatory framework might indicate. While the Ministry of National Economy of the Republic of Kazakhstan (MNE) provides some central guidance and oversight of the development of strategic plans and budget programs, in practice responsibility for the definition of programs, performance indicators, and targets is largely devolved to line ministries and agencies, resulting in an uneven quality of the strategic plans and the design of budget programs. Overall, while Kazakhstan performs relatively well in visioning for results, it needs to further improve its results-based budgeting, implementation, and monitoring systems.

It is important for the government to maintain the current Sustainable Development Goals (SDGs) momentum to increase the pace of attaining the SDGs. There is an opportunity to connect the ongoing process of nationalizing and localizing the SDG indicators with the authorities' endeavors to improve the monitoring of progress against the national development targets and how state spending contributes to these development outcomes.

This requires the nationalized and localized SDG indicators to be mainstreamed into the State Planning System and its monitoring mechanism. This process constitutes a critical step to facilitate the alignment of the planning processes with the budgetary processes in Kazakhstan. It would enable the stronger integration of Kazakhstan's planning and financing processes and initiate the progress toward establishing an Integrated National Financing Framework (INFF) to strengthen the country's SDG financing mechanisms.

While there are formal rules and mechanisms in place to facilitate participation of civil society and businesses in decision-making, the prevailing impression is that the changes in the decision-making process have thus far been more formal than actual. The planning system and control from the central

Table 1. Headline Recommendation: Develop a Holistic Financing Strategy

HEADLINE FINDINGS	RECOMMENDATIONS
1. Stagnation of total available development finance 2. Increasing reliance on domestic sources of finance, including domestic commercial investments with a significant share of state-related private sector investment 3. Tensions between long-term fiscal sustainability and social spending 4. Trade-offs between development priorities and financing policies and instruments 5. Disconnect between the long-term development vision and short-term financing policies	Lay out a holistic financing strategy to raise resources, manage risks, and achieve sustainable development priorities: • Estimate resource needs of the development strategy Kazakhstan-2050 and for the 2030 Agenda • Establish financing targets for both public and private resources to meet identified resource needs • Integrate a "Development finance assessment Dashboard (DFA Dashboard)" in the Forecast of Social and Economic Development (FSED) • Access untapped sources of climate-related development finance • Reform fossil fuel subsidies • Streamline tax incentives and exemptions according to cost-benefit analyses

administration leave limited room for maneuver to the ministries to accommodate multi-stakeholder consultations.

Table 2 summarizes the recommendations to strengthen the linkages between the state planning system, the budgeting process and the SDGs.

In conclusion, the overarching, headline recommendation that emerges from this initial, light development finance assessment (DFA) analysis would be for Kazakhstan to consider the value of developing an INFF to strengthen the financing of its long-term sustainable development strategy. Kazakhstan's development finance landscape and outlook has changed significantly in the recent decade. Now is the time to adapt its financing policies toward maximizing the development impact of its public spending and attract an increasing share of international development finance. Several INFF across both DFA dimensions analyzed point to the potential usefulness of adopting an INFF to both maximize development finance as well as inform strategic resource allocations toward achieving development results. The two key areas of recommendations that are developed in more detail in this report focus on strengthening the institutional structures and required building blocks toward developing an INFF.

Table 2. Headline Recommendation: Strengthen the Sustainable Development Goal Financing Mechanisms

HEADLINE FINDINGS	RECOMMENDATIONS
1. Weak links between planning and budgeting processes 2. Unclear how public spending contributes to progress against the Sustainable Development Goals (SDGs) 3. Uneven implementation of results-based budgeting across ministries 4. Low quality of the key performance indicators for the budget programs planning documents 5. Strategic planning remains largely top-down, with limited, effective contributions by civil society and business	Strengthen linkages between the state planning system, the budgeting process, and the SDGs: • Integrate the nationalized SDG indicators across state planning system and the budget process • Introduce SDG budgeting • Broadening participation of non-state actors in the budget or policy development process

Introduction

The 2030 Agenda presents an ambitious, complex, and interconnected vision that countries around the world have committed to working toward. Realizing this vision will require mobilizing a diverse range of public and private resources to contribute to sustainable development outcomes and achieving the Sustainable Development Goals (SDGs). Meanwhile, significant changes are taking place in the development finance landscape worldwide—traditional donors now share the space with emerging donors, foundations, and the private sector, among others.

Countries face several challenges in developing an integrated approach to financing the SDGs. Mobilizing the scale of public and private resources required while maximizing their impact on social, environmental, and economic dimensions of the 2030 Agenda presents a range of challenges, from managing complex financing instruments, to designing and implementing effective policies, and collaborating with a diverse range of actors. These challenges are often rooted in, or made more difficult by, misalignment between the planning and finance policy functions of government, as well as the participation of only a narrow group of stakeholders in dialogue and decisions on financing.

Kazakhstan is strongly committed to achieving the SDGs and is setting itself up to deliver on the 2030 Agenda. With the support of the Asian Development Bank (ADB) and the United Nations Development Programme (UNDP) it has established a Coordination Board on Sustainable Development Goals. It is chaired by the deputy prime minister, with the Ministry of National Economy (MNE) as coordinating body. Five SDG Working Groups were formed in accordance with the five "P" principles underpinning the SDGs (Peace, People, Planet, Prosperity and Partnership). The Economic Research Institute under the MNE (ERI) as the secretariat provide analytical support to the SDG Working Groups. Similarly, the National Committee on Statistics will support the SDGs implementation monitoring process. On 16 July 2019, Kazakhstan presented its first Voluntary National Review (VNR) at the High-Level Political Forum in New York. It is now in the process of nationalizing and localizing the SDG targets.

This development finance assessment (DFA) informs the government's efforts toward the 2030 Agenda by informing their approach toward strengthening their SDG financing mechanisms. Member states of the United Nations recognized the challenge of SDG financing in the Addis Ababa Action Agenda. They decided to put in place the Integrated National Financing Framework (INFF) to support their sustainable development strategies. The UNDP developed several tools to analyze existing financial resources and identify opportunities to mobilize additional sources of finance more efficiently to achieve the SDGs, including the DFA.

A DFA supports governments and their partners in identifying and building consensus around solutions to address financing challenges. It makes finance issues accessible to policy and decision makers. It follows a process of a multi-stakeholder consultation informed by accessible analysis on finance policy issues and what they mean for a wide range of actors and builds an agreed road map that can support progress across a range of areas. Figure 1 illustrates the five dimensions of a DFA.

This report addresses both the first and second dimensions of a DFA. These analyze the development finance landscape of both public and private available resources and the integration and alignment between the planning and financing processes in Kazakhstan. As such, this exercise is a lighter version of the full analysis, which would require more time, resources and in-depth exchanges with the country's policy makers and development stakeholders. This exercise serves the purpose of warming up the government and its development partners to the idea of undertaking a complete DFA or consider developing INFFs. Therefore, this report suggests an initial set of recommendations that constitute initial steps toward implementing the INFF building blocks and strengthen Kazakhstan's SDG financing mechanism.

The report is structured according to the DFA dimensions. The first chapter explores Kazakhstan's financing landscape. It focuses primarily on the past decade, starting from 2008 in line with the availability of official data. Chapter two describes the current state planning system and how it aligns with the budgetary processes. It compares the formal, de jure institutional set-up, according to government legislation, with the de facto planning and budgetary practices, based on available, recent expert analysis and consultations with government stakeholders. The third and final chapter suggests priority areas for improvement, based on the previous analysis.

Figure 1. Dimensions of a Development Finance Assessment

Dimension 1: Assessing the Development Finance Landscape

Finance has a critical role to play in delivering the Strategy Kazakhstan-2050 and the 2030 Agenda. Kazakhstan will need to mobilize the right scale and mix of all resources—public and private, domestic and international—while maximizing synergies and minimizing risks. The 2019 Financing for Sustainable Development Report recommends countries to consider developing INFFs to support their national development strategies. Many countries use DFAs as the basis for developing an INFF road map. Developing an INFF supports shifting financing perspectives toward long-term investment horizons and integrating sustainability as a central concern of investment decisions. It enables aligning private and public incentives with sustainable development, and better measuring the impacts on sustainability.

This chapter covers the first dimension of the DFA. This first dimension of the analytical framework analyzes financing trends within the country. It builds as comprehensive a picture as possible of public and private resources, flows, and financial instruments. First, it provides the full picture of all available development finance flows. Then it discusses separately available public resources, followed by an analysis of private resources and actors. The findings from this chapter may directly support developing an INFF's first building block assessment and diagnostics.

CURRENT TRENDS IN THE DEVELOPMENT FINANCE LANDSCAPE

Kazakhstan's development finance landscape is mitigated. Figure 2 indicates how the total available amount of development finance increased steadily up until 2015, up until the decline of international oil prices. The increase in total development finance has not kept pace with the country's gross domestic product (GDP) growth, however, resulting in declining development finance as a share of GDP. Development finance peaked at 64% of GDP in 2010, after which it declined to an average 39% of GDP in 2018.

Since development needs are likely to increase as economies develop, this forebodes a challenging financing environment for the near future in a business -as- usual scenario. It is therefore critical to mobilize and channel scarce available resources into investments that will yield sustainable development results, all the while undertaking the necessary policy actions now to revert the downward trend towards ustainably increasing financial resources. Left unchecked, this may constrain the ability to achieve development outcomes results.

This overview of the development finance landscape includes the amount of annual oil tax revenues that accrue to the National Fund of the Republic of Kazakhstan[1] (NFRK) (Figure 3). While this revenue may not be directly available to the authorities for funding public services and investments, it does represent development finance that eventually serves a clear policy purpose of intergenerational savings and stabilization. The resource extractive activity that generates these oil-related tax revenues are also included in the GDP figures. Therefore, excluding the oil-related tax revenues that are a not transferred

---

[1] The government of Kazakhstan created the NFRK in 2000 to manage oil revenue more effectively. The NFRK operates as both a stabilization and a savings fund.

Figure 2. Total Available Development Finance

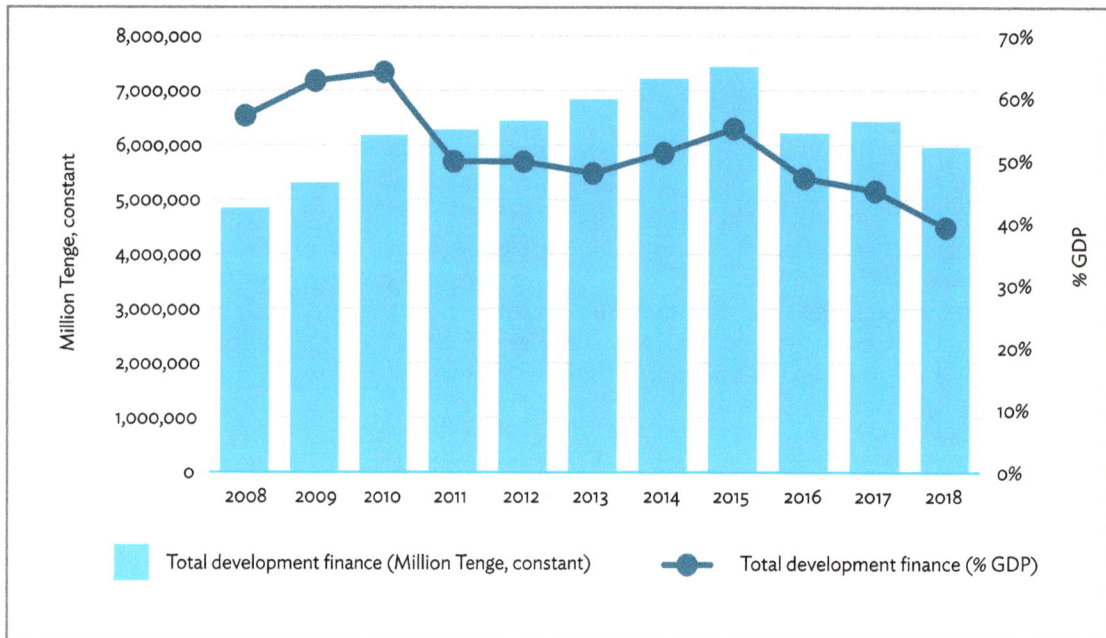

GDP = gross domestic product: Author's calculations based on Ministry of Finance of Kazakhstan, National Bank of Kazakhstan, Organisation for Economic Co-operation and Development, World Bank.

Figure 3. Development Finance Landscape 2008-2018

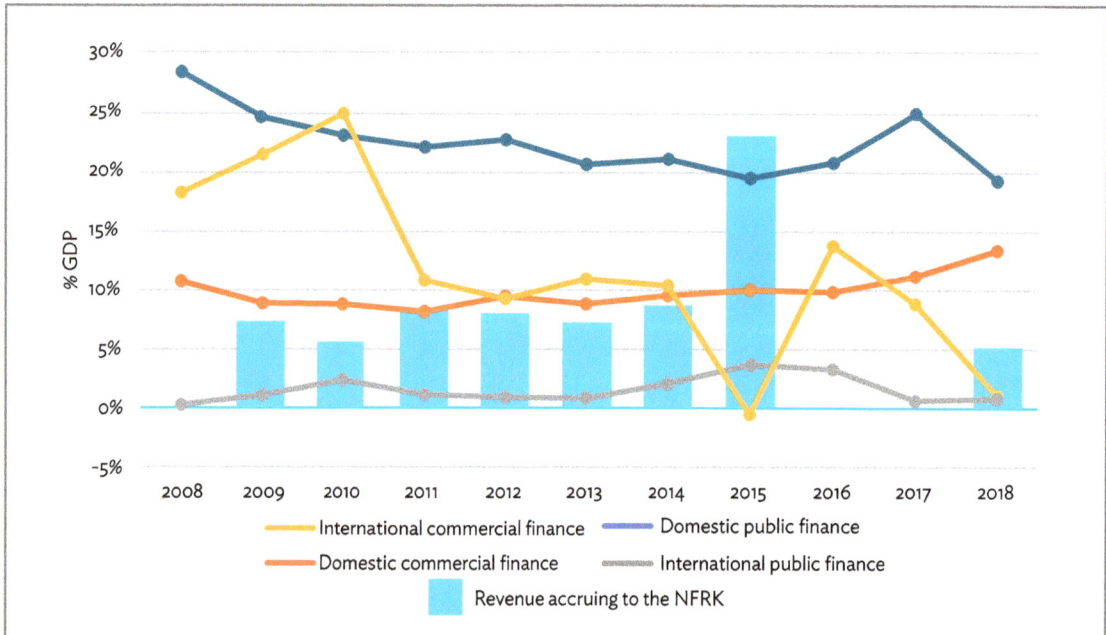

GDP = gross domestic product, NFRK = National Fund of the Republic of Kazakhstan.
Sources: Own calculations based on Ministry of Finance of the Republic of Kazakhstan, National Bank of Kazakhstan, Organisation for Economic Co-operation and Development, World Bank.

automatically to the state budget would distort the total development finance picture as a share of GDP

Going forward, the analysis of government revenue involves only the non-oil tax revenues (including customs revenue from oil export) and the NFRK transfers to the state budget, as these are the financial resource that the government can dispose to implement its policy objectives.

During the past decade, domestic finance, both public and commercial, has dominated Kazakhstan's financing landscape. It averaged 31.6% of GDP during the past 5 years (2014–2018). In comparison, international finance only averaged 8.7% of GDP over the same period.[2] This marks a stark departure from the reliance on international commercial financial resources, mostly FDI, that fueled the country's socioeconomic development since its independence until 2010.

Recent international commercial finance flows to Kazakhstan mark two periods of sharp declines: in 2011 following the onset of the global economic crisis and in 2015, following the oil price decline.[3] The relative decline in international commercial finances to Kazakhstan is one of the headline findings from this DFA.

International public finance constitutes the smallest component of Kazakhstan's development landscape, averaging only 2.1 of GDP for 2014–2018. The slight increase during 2015 and 2016 represents an uptake in external public debt.

The volatility of international private finance, following the end of the resource super cycle and global economic slowdown, translates into volatile total amount of available development finance for Kazakhstan. This volatility complicates adopting a long-term horizon for planning the contribution of international investments to development outcomes in areas most suited to benefit from international investments, like infrastructure projects. The NFRK served its purpose of promoting macroeconomic stability during the post-2007 global financial crisis. However, the new normal of low oil prices since 2014 has reduced the value of Kazakhstan's oil wealth. Achieving long-term fiscal sustainability and intergenerational equity, therefore, may enter in conflict with short term, pressing needs to address short-term volatility in oil revenues.

Unpacking total available finance to Kazakhstan into its different components confirms the critical contribution of government revenue to the country's development outcomes (Figure 4). The compound annual growth rate of government revenue was 2.4% since 2008. While this represents an increase in absolute value (Figure 5), relative to GDP the amount of available government revenue declined from 25% in 2008 to 17.5% in 2018. This implies that available government revenue grew at a slower pace than the growth of the economy. Government revenue comprises mainly tax revenues, nontax revenues and transfers from the NFRK.

This DFA finds that the only financing flow that increased significantly during 2008–2018 is domestic commercial investment. Since 2008 it has grown at a compound rate of 8%, albeit starting from a lower base. As a share of GDP, the increase is less marked, nevertheless it stands out as it is the only finance flow that increased. Domestic commercial investments represent investments in fixed assets of households and the private sector as provided by NBK data.

---

[2] An important analytical aspect that would warrant more in-depth analysis in the follow-up to this light DFA is the risk of double counting international and private financial flows (e.g., loans attracted from abroad are counted as international development finance, and then their on-lending in the form of bank credits to domestic banks is counted as domestic development finance).

[3] Crude oil prices collapsed from $108.76/barrel in September 2013 to $47.11/barrel in January 2015.

Figure 4. Relative Contribution of Main finance Components in Total Available Development Finance

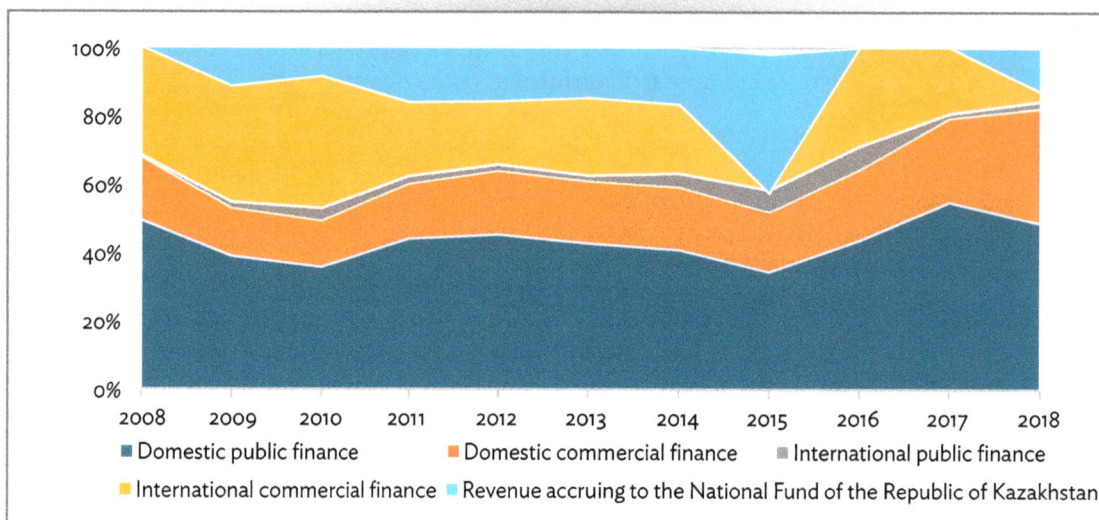

Sources: Own calculations based on Ministry of Finance of the Republic of Kazakhstan, National Bank of Kazakhstan, Organisation for Economic Co-operation and Development, World Bank.

Figure 5. Evolution of Development Finance Flows in Kazakhstan

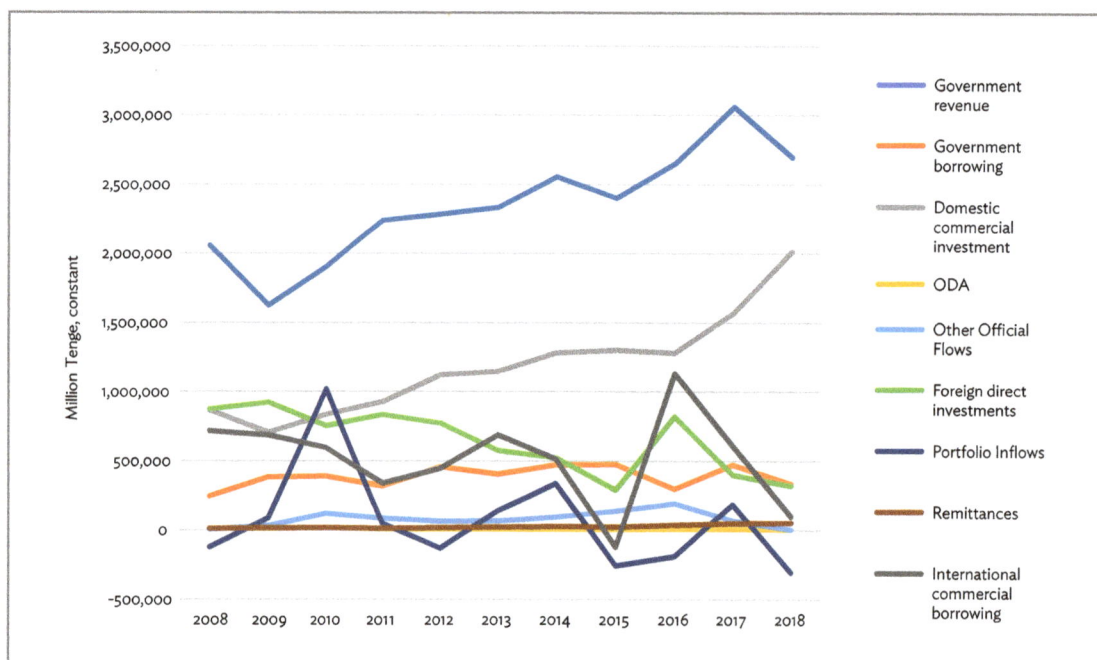

ODA = official development assistance.
Sources: Own calculations based on Ministry of Finance of the Republic of Kazakhstan, National Bank of Kazakhstan, Organisation for Economic Co-operation and Development, World Bank.
Notes: Total development finance here includes revenue - oil revenue and investment income from the National Fund management - accruing to the the National Fund of the Republic of Kazakstan (NFRK). No NFRK data for 2008 and no revenue accruing to the NFRK in 2016 and 2017.

Figure 6. Evolution of Development Finance Flows in Kazakhstan as a Share of Gross Domestic Product

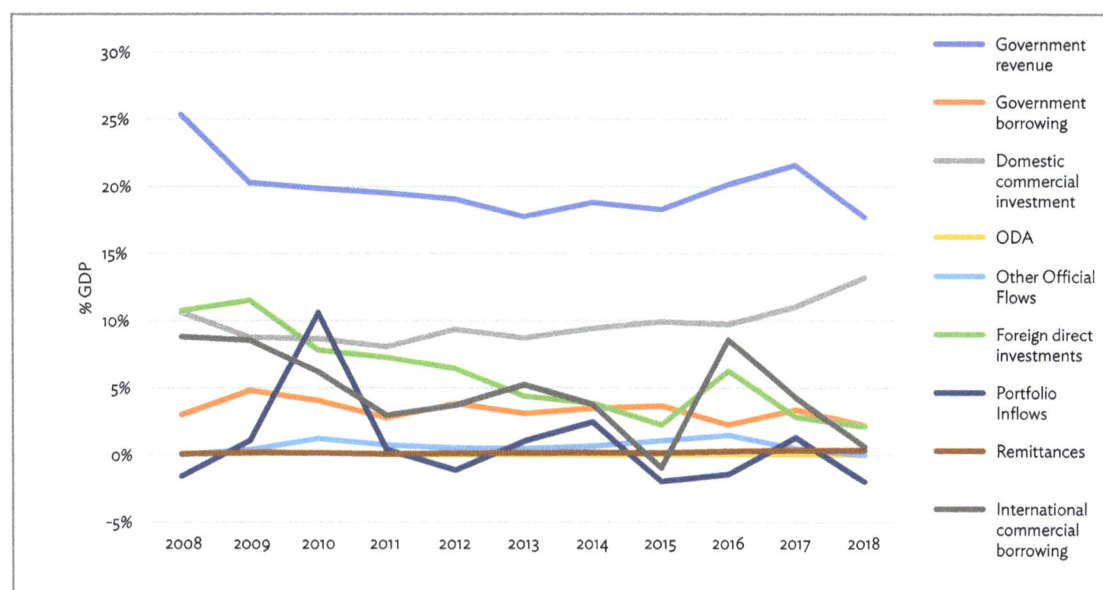

ODA = official development assistance.
Sources: Own calculations based on Ministry of Finance of the Republic of Kazakhstan, National Bank of Kazakhstan, Organisation for Economic Co-operation and Development, World Bank
Notes: Total development finance here includes revenue - oil revenue and investment income from the National Fund management- accruing to the National Fund of the Republic of Kazakstan (NFRK).. No NFRK data for 2008 and no revenue accruing to the NFRK in 2016 and 2017.

International private finance mostly comprises FDI. FDI underpinned Kazakhstan's economic growth boom, averaging levels of 8.6% of GDP in 2005–2010, compared to 4.4% for 2011–2018, according to NBK data. Foreign private investment played a critical role in expanding Kazakhstan's infrastructure stock and its resource extractive industry.

This review of development finance trends in Kazakhstan's points to the following considerations:

• The importance of maximizing the developmental impact of available domestic public finance, considering it is the major source of available finance. Strategies to do so may include improving spending efficiency, avoiding future costs, or realigning spending.

• Strengthen the buoyancy of the current tax system to ensure government revenue increases more than GDP growth. Such an approach involves both improving tax collection efficiency and reviewing fiscal policy.

• Incentivize domestic commercial investment so it aligns with Kazakhstan's national sustainable development priorities and the SDGs. A thriving domestic private sector is essential to further increase the country's living standards through productive employment and higher wages.

• In-depth analysis of how to attract an increasing amount of international commercial investments toward the non-resource sectors to speed up the economy's structural transformation.

DOMESTIC AND INTERNATIONAL PUBLIC FINANCE

Public finance comprises government revenue, public borrowing, official development assistance (ODA) and other official flows. Kazakhstan is an upper middle-income country, so it receives very little ODA. It does receive official funding from international financial institutions (IFIs) under the concept of other official flows and nonconcessional lending. In contrast to commercial flows, the government can control how to allocate its available public finance in line with its strategic development priorities.

Total public finance to Kazakhstan declined from its peak of 28.3% of GDP in 2008 to a low of 19.9% of GDP in 2018 (Figure 7). Public borrowing and other official flows remained stable at an average of respectively 3.3% and 0.6% of GDP over the same period 2008–2018. Therefore, the past decade's decline in available public finance can almost exclusively be attributed to declining government revenue as a share of GDP – the latter having been offset by increasing transfers from the NFRK for the years 2015, 2016, and 2017.

Government Revenue and Public Borrowing

In 2018, government revenue represented 89% of total public finance. The remainder consisted of public borrowing, both internal and external, to finance the fiscal deficit (Table 3). Government revenue has been declining as a share of GDP, from 25.1% of GDP in 2008 to 17.5% in 2018. Government revenue represented $1,716 per capita in 2018, down from a peak of $2,462 per capita in 2013. To give a sense of these figures, average government revenues per person of $940 across the Association of Southeast Asian Nations (ASEAN) region compare with over $15,000 per person in high-income countries (Development Initiatives, 2015). The declining trend in available government revenue per capita signals the need to tap into additional sources of funding, public debt or commercial investments, to enable

Figure 7. Composition of Public Finance Flows

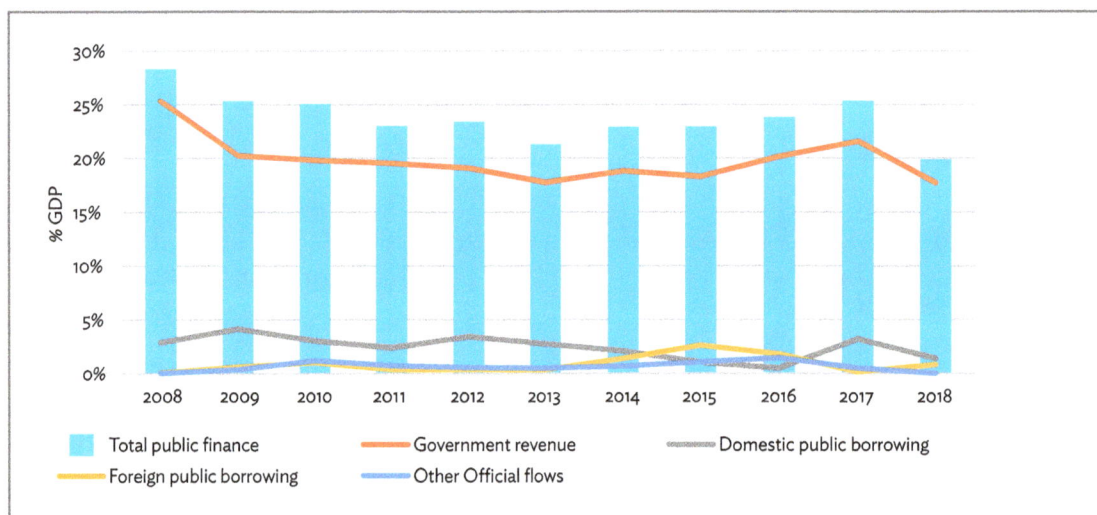

GDP = gross domestic product.
Sources: Ministry of Finance of the Republic of Kazakhstan, National Bank of Kazakhstan, Organisation for Economic Co-operation and Development, World Bank.

Table 3. Overview of Government Revenue and Public Borrowing

In billion tenge, current	2008	2009	2010	2011	2012	2013	2014	2015	2016	2017	2018
Government revenue (I)	4,064	3,443	4,324	5,508	5,907	6,383	7,454	7,466	9,452	11,719	10,939
Tax revenues	2,820	2,229	2,934	3,982	4,095	4,779	5,116	4,884	6,023	6,811	7,890
Non-tax revenues	86	136	104	139	285	142	179	225	369	274	226
Proceeds from the sale of fixed capital	57	36	61	50	52	56	71	70	60	69	93
NFRK transfers receipts	1,072	1,105	1,200	1,200	1,380	1,406	1,955	2,456	2,856	4,414	2,600
Other revenue	30	(63)	25	138	94	1	133	(168)	143	151	131
Government borrowing (II)	477	809	882	780	1,179	1,103	1,366	1,479	1,055	1,805	1,347
Domestic Government Loans	465	708	660	674	1,068	983	827	420	218	1,733	853
Foreign Government Loans	12	102	222	106	111	121	539	1,060	836	72	494
TOTAL (I)+(II)	4,541	4,252	5,206	6,288	7,085	7,486	8,820	8,946	0,506	13,524	12,286
TOTAL (Billion $, current)	37.8	28.8	35.3	42.9	47.5	49.2	49.2	40.3	30.7	41.5	35.6
Revenue accruing to the NFRK		1,235	1,208	2,288	2,464	2,586	3,412	9,337	...	...	3,156

NFRK = National Fund of the Republic of Kazakhstan, ... = Not available.
Source: Ministry of Finance of the Republic of Kazakhstan.

maintaining the same levels of public service. Increasing public debt, however, should be realized considering prudent or sustainable management of country's total external debt, including SOE borrowing.

The central government budget relies on annual guaranteed transfers from the NFRK, which amount to $8 billion plus or minus 15% depending on the phase of the economic cycle (OECD, 2017). Tax revenue comprised 73% and NFRK 24% of total government revenue in 2018 (Figure 8). NFRK transfers averaged 28% during 2008–2018. This share increased to 32% in 2015, 31% in 2016 and 38% in 2017, following the authorities' decision to finance countercyclical measures using NFRK reserves.

The central government budget relies on annual guaranteed transfers from the NFRK, which amount to $8 billion plus or minus 15% depending on the phase of the economic cycle (OECD, 2017). Tax revenue and NFRK transfers comprised respectively 73% and 24% of total government revenue in 2018 (Figure 8 below). NFRK transfers averaged 28% during 2008-2018. This share increased to 32% in 2015, 31% in 2016 and 38% in 2017, following the authorities' decision to finance countercyclical measures using

Figure 8. Composition of Government Revenue

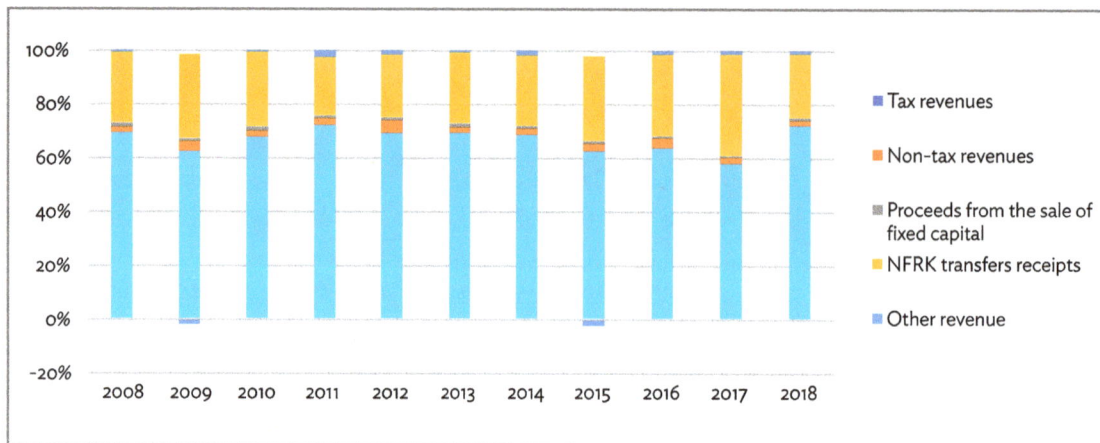

NFRK = National Fund of the Republic of Kazakhstan.
Source: Ministry of Finance of the Republic of Kazakhstan.

NFRK reserves. Targeted transfers can be made by presidential decree for socially significant projects if alternative funding sources are insufficient. For example, during 2014-2015, targeted transfers of $5.4 billion were made mainly to support the recovery of the banking sector, to provide bank lending to small and medium-sized enterprises (SMEs) and to finance infrastructure projects. For 2015–2017, annual transfers of $3 billion supported sustainable economic growth and employment within the new State Program of Infrastructure Development (Nurly Zhol). As a result, the total available amount of NFRK reserves decreased by 11% from their peak of T25,754 billion in 2015 to T22,925 billion in 2017. Figure 9 illustrates how the decrease of the NRFK was driven by the combination of a strong decrease in NFRK receipts following the oil price shock and the increase in NFRK expenditure.

Figure 9. Evolution of the National Fund of the Republic of Kazakhstan Reserves

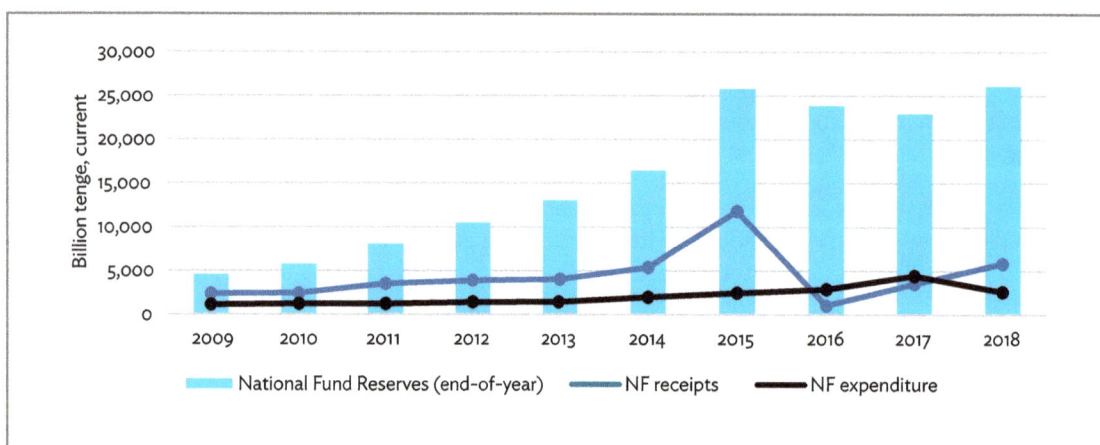

NF = National Fund
Source: Ministry of Finance of the Republic of Kazakhstan

Box 1. The Evolution of the National Fund of the Republic of Kazakhstan Reserves Provide the Collateral for International Borrowing

Clear fiscal objectives, including legally grounded fiscal rules, are helpful to governments seeking to pursue a sound and sustainable fiscal policy. Well formulated rules, and the government's adherence to them, strengthen the government's credibility. In resource-rich countries such as Kazakhstan, such rules can also help to ensure that natural resource endowments are used prudently.

In parallel, a new "Concept for the Formation and Use of the National Fund" was adopted in 2016 and implemented in 2018, with the aim of stabilizing the National Fund of the Republic of Kazakhstan (NFRK) and reducing budgetary dependence on oil revenues, which have in the past accounted for more than 40% of total budget revenues. It establishes several rules regarding maintenance of the NFRK and the size of transfers to the budget as follows:

1. Upper monetary limit on the amount that can be transferred from the National Fund to the republican budget (KZT 2,000 billion per annum by 2020).

2. The total value of the NFRK should not drop below 30% of GDP.

3. Total public debt, including the debt of state-owned enterprises, should not exceed the assets of the NFRK.

4. Annual expenditures on public debt service do not exceed 4.5% of assets managed.

Eventually, managing the NFRK is about striking a balance between sound fiscal management of the country's oil reserves to achieve its stabilization and savings function and assuaging Kazakhstan's resource needs to finance pressing investments, which may yield important socio-economic returns. These new rules, adapted to the changed international economic environment, signal the government's intention of stricter fiscal management of its oil wealth. It is important to avoid a gap between what the rules say and how fiscal policy is run, for example by adopting formal mechanisms, subject to parliamentary approval, to allow for discretionary spending of oil wealth in case of need or to relax some of the austerity implied by the rules.

Source: OECD, 2017; OECD, 2019.

Both the real and perceived risk of a depletion of NFRK reserves may negatively impact on the country's borrowing capacity and its cost on international financial markets (Box 1.). According to International Monetary Fund (IMF, 2017) calculations, the government's net financial assets—the difference between NFRK assets and total accumulated government debt—would fall close to zero by 2021 under a business-as-usual scenario (Figure 10).

In addition to the quantity of reserves, the quality of governance of the NFRK also matters to signal the authorities' commitment to long-term sustainable management of the NFRK. The recent increase in discretionary spending of NFRK reserves to bail out major private banks and to fund countercyclical policies may signal that the new fiscal rules to manage the use of the NFRK funds may end up being circumvented. To maximize the NFRK funds' developmental impact, may want to consider additional

Figure 10. Kazakhstan: Net Financial Assets (in % of GDP)

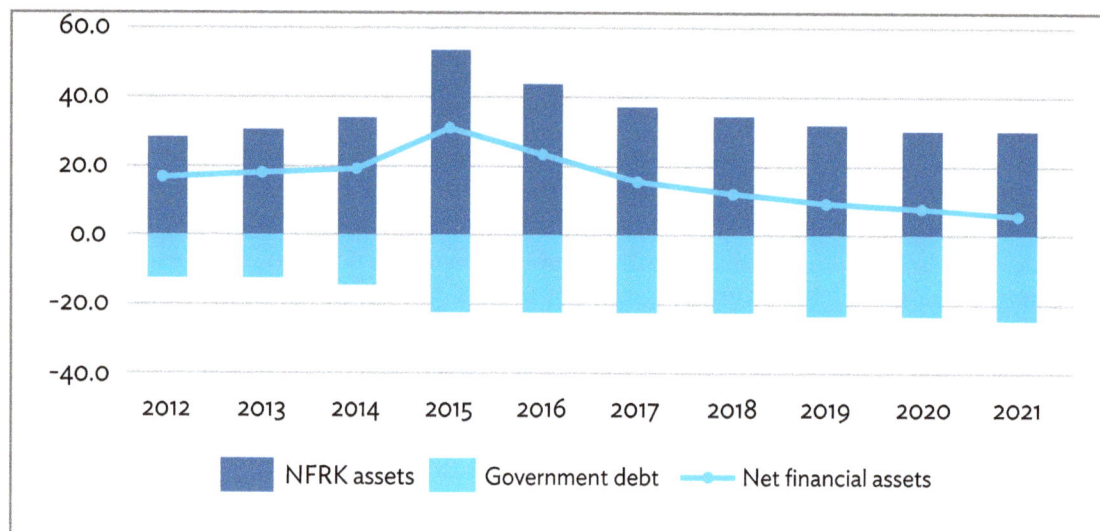

GDP = gross domestic product, NFRK = National Fund of the Republic of Kazakhstan.
Source: International Monetary Fund, 2017.

mechanisms to ensure the value-for-money of fund allocations, such as projects that would benefit underdeveloped regions or vulnerable segments of the population.

Considering the new normal of a low-oil prices environment[4] Kazakhstan needs to urgently adopt a fiscal consolidation strategy to promote diversified growth and high-quality job creation. The World Bank highlights two important approaches to underpin this successful fiscal consolidation: "reducing inefficient expenditure that distorts private incentives while redirecting savings toward productivity-enhancing spending; and eliminating inefficient tax benefits that result in an uneven playing field for investment." (World Bank, 2018). The potential for increasing tax collections by eliminating exemptions and closing tax loopholes is significant. According to government estimates, in 2016 the combined revenue cost of tax expenditures for corporate income tax (CIT) and value-added tax (VAT) was almost T3 trillion (6% of GDP) (World Bank, 2017). Such measures should be informed by analyzing the macro-implications on demand, through their impact on household incomes and employment. Using appropriate thresholds for the application of VAT exemptions may be considered to protect vulnerable groups from tax hikes. Ideally, any tax reforms should be informed by an analysis of the measures fiscal incidence, combining both revenue and spending measures.

Importantly, both the World Bank recommendations refer to how Kazakhstan's public spending policies are indirectly undermining the private sector's contribution to the country's socioeconomic development. Failure to consolidate would result in the precipitated depletion of net fiscal savings of the NFRK in less than a generation.[5] According to authorities, fiscal consolidation is expected to resume starting 2020 with the goal to reduce non-oil deficit to 5.4% of GDP in 2022 from over 8% of GDP in 2019.

---

[4] Presentation made by Alexander Van De Putte at the Regional SDG Summit 2019 in Almaty.

[5] Ato Brown. 2018 World Bank Country Manager for Kazakhstan, 12 January https://www.worldbank.org/en/news/opinion/2018/01/12/supporting-kazakhstans-commitmentto-fiscal-consolidation-and-long-term-economic-transformation.

In this context, authorities face limited choices to increase public investments or social spending. There is a trade-off between further using debt financing to bridge the fiscal deficit, which comes at a financial cost, or using additional NFRK, which is limited by the new fiscal rules. Urgent measures are required to compensate the gradual decrease of transfers for the NFRK to the state budget by increasing tax and non-tax revenue.

The reliance on easy resource rents and oil tax revenue to fund the state budget may have delayed necessary reforms to increase non-oil tax revenues. According to a 2012 study by the World Bank, there is significant potential to increase tax revenues in Kazakhstan. They estimated Kazakhstan's tax effort at 0.50 for the period 2002–2009, which implies the country collecting less than what it could reasonably be expected to collect given the structural determinants of its economy.[6] They predicted a tax ratio of 26.15% of GDP, compared to the then ratio of 14.6% of GDP. The issues behind the low tax effort are manifold, including generous tax exemptions eroding the tax base in combination with low tax rates and ineffective tax administration.

Table 4. Caucasus and Central Asia Non-Oil Tax Collection Efficiency, 2015 (%, 100 is best)

	Value-added Tax Efficiency[a]	Corporate Income Tax Collection Efficiency[b]
Kazakhstan	35	16
Uzbekistan	57	43
Georgia	93	22
Tajikistan	62	...
Upper-middle-income countries	58	17

Note: ... = data not available. Tajikistan and Turkmenistan partly omitted due to missing data.
[a]VAT Efficiency – VAT revenue divided by the product of VAT rate and total private consumption.
[b]CIT Collection Efficiency – CIT to GDP ratio divided by the CIT rate; Azerbaijan, Kazakhstan, and Turkmenistan show non-oil CIT efficiency.
Sources: IMF Fiscal Affairs Department tax database 2017; World Enconomic Outlook 2017; KPMG; and IMF staff calculations.

According to government data, tax revenues[7] declined from 17.6% in 2008 to 12.8% in 2018. The period's average of 13.1% of GDP compares low to other upper middle-income countries (UMICs) and even low-income countries (LICs). Part of this decline relates to lower customs revenue from oil exports from 2014 onward. Also, tax collection efficiency of (VAT and corporate income tax is lower than comparators in Kazakhstan (Table 4) (IMF, 2018b). The volatility of Kazakhstan's oil-related tax revenue impacts its revenue mobilization and the ability to plan public investment.

Kazakhstan compares favorably to its neighboring peers and UMICs on the paying taxes indicators. It has significantly reduced the time to prepare and pay taxes since 2010, but fares a little worse in the numbers of tax payments to be made (Table 5).

Kazakhstan's tax mix is dominated by corporate income taxes, VAT and trade taxes, together representing close to 80% of the tax take in 2018 (Figure 11). Of all oil-related revenues, only the proceeds of the oil export customs duty go directly to the state budget.

---

[6] The ratio of the actual tax collection to the predicted tax revenue (taxable capacity).

[7] Tax revenues here don't include oil related taxes, which go straight to the NFRK, with the exception of customs revenue from oil export.

Table 5. Evolution of the World Bank Paying Taxes Indicators

	Total Tax and Contribution Rate (% of profit)		Tax Payments (number)		Corporate Income Tax Collection Efficiency	
	2010	2019	2010	2019	2010	2019
Upper middle income	39.6	39.1	33	21	297	284
Europe and Central Asia (excluding high income)	40.1	32.5	53	14	346	226
Kazakhstan	29.8	28.4	8	10	261	186
Georgia	15.3	9.9	30	5	387	216
Azerbaijan	38.9	40.7	18	9	165	159

Source: World Bank. 2019. World Development Indicators. Washington, DC.
http://datatopics.worldbank.org/world-development-indicators/

Figure 11. Kazakhstan's Tax Mix

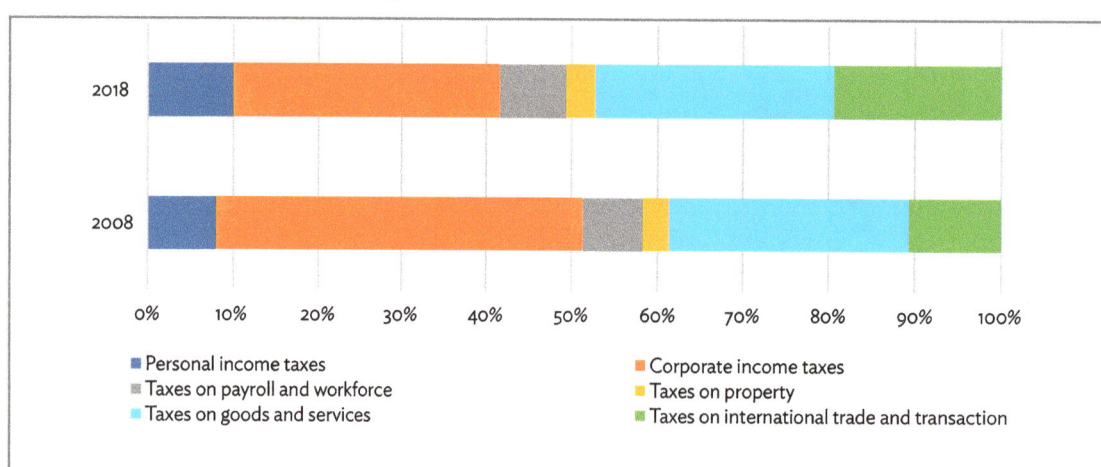

Source: ADB. 2019. Key Indicators for Asia and the Pacific. Manila. https://www.adb.org/publications/key-indicators-asia-and-pacific-2019

The increasing share of indirect taxes in Kazakhstan's total tax mix points to an increasingly regressive tax system. Indirect taxes increased from representing 41% in 2008 to 47% in 2018. Indirect taxes do not look at the consumer's ability to pay, but are the same for everyone who buys the goods or services. The authorities' plan to reduce the personal income tax (PIT) rate for low-income earners is therefore positive; to further enhance progressivity, a moderate increase of PIT rates for high-income earners could be considered.

The finding that Kazakhstan's tax take is decreasing and significantly below potential in addition to its tax system being regressive, warrants urgent consideration by the government. The IMF[8] identifies reforms and new opportunities may offer potential for higher rates of growth in revenue, including tax

---

[8] IMF website July 2019

administration gains from the VAT and enhanced technology; tax policy changes to support higher non-oil revenues and improve equity, introducing progressive income and property taxes and reviewing widespread exemptions from VAT and CIT. The 2017 World Bank Public Finance Review estimates that these exemptions reduce revenue by about 20% of the yield of these taxes, or 1.3% of GDP in 2016. Rapid revenue gains are difficult, but not impossible on the condition of the political will of government to take politically costly, but financially inexpensive, reform steps of proven efficacy to improve enforcement. (See example of Georgia's successful tax reforms in Box 2). A practical proxy of political commitment to tax enforcement is the extent to which the data held by other public agencies that would be useful to the tax agency is made available to that agency.[9]

Box 2. Cracking Down on Corruption Combined with Digital Technology Enabled Rapid, Sustained Revenue Increases in Georgia

Following its 2003 'Rose Revolution', Georgia's new government embarked on an aggressive agenda of legal, regulatory, and institutional reforms designed to stamp out public sector corruption, increase tax collection and create an attractive environment for business investment. In 2003, tax collection stood at only 12% of gross domestic product (GDP). The administrative burdens and compliance costs for taxpayers was high and significant public sector corruption undermined citizen's trust in government and taxpayers' willingness to pay taxes.

In 2004, sweeping reforms purged the administration of many corrupt practices, replacing the entire police force, as well as most tax and customs officers. Corrupt practices were no longer tolerated and some tax officers were prosecuted and jailed.

Between 2004 and 2009, the State Revenue Service (SRS) strengthened tax collection by streamlining and automating most processes, introducing risk-based audit management and vastly expanding e-services. This simplified taxpayer requirements and greatly reduced face-to-face time between tax officers and taxpayers. The Ministry of Finance introduced electronic information sharing between the Georgian Revenue Service, taxpayers, banks, and other authorities. This was done in combination with aggressive implementation of improvements, such as e-filing of taxes, a one-stop internet portal and electronic taxpayer registration.

As a result, total tax receipts soared from only 12% of GDP to 25% between 2003 and 2012, despite declining tax receipts on international trade due to the slashing of import duty rates. The number of registered taxpayers more than doubled between 2005 and 2008: meanwhile, value-added tax (VAT) revenues rose from 8.5% of GDP in 2005 to 11.3% in 2009. E-filing of all tax obligations, which took off from barely any e-filings in 2008 to 800,000 in 2009, accounting for 76% of total revenue and lowering compliance costs. The tax administration reforms and anti-corruption measures have led to a drastic fall in the number of bribery cases involving tax officials.

Source: International Tax Compact (ITC) & OECD, 2015.

---

[9] Bird R. 2019. Review of new World Bank framework "Innovations in Tax Compliance". ICTD Blog published 12 November.

> ### Box 3. Fiscal Policy for Health
>
> Tobacco, alcohol, and sugary beverage consumption accounts for a large and growing share of premature death and disease, especially in low- and middle- income countries. Raising the price of tobacco, alcohol and sugary beverages – so-called 'sin taxes'– by increasing excise taxes reduces consumption and saves lives, while generating additional tax revenues.
>
> Excise taxes on sugar and sweetened beverages may be a relevant health policy in Kazakhstan to contain future health expenditure from diabetes and obesity. In Kazakhstan, almost 20% of children aged 6 to 9 years suffer from excessive weight or obesity that is mostly a result of unhealthy eating habits and insufficient physical activity. Obesity is most common in children from high-income families or with relatively few children and is often linked to excessive consumption of sugar, sweets, commercial sweet drinks, saturated fats and trans fatty acids.
>
> The 2012 Philippines' 'sin tax reform'-restructuring excise tax on alcohol and tobacco- ended a precipitous decline in the value of excise taxes on alcohol and tobacco caused by loopholes in previous legislation. Under the new law, revenues increased year-on-year by 85.6%, yielding fresh revenue of some ₱51 billion (approximately, $1.18 billion) in 2013. Close to 80% of this figure is earmarked to health-care subsidies for the poorest Filipinos. The legislation was made both technically sound and politically smart through a process involving a network of players within and outside government, including campaigning by civil society around the public health dimension.
>
> *Sources: UN CCA, Bloomberg Task Force on Fiscal Policy for Health, Booth (2014).*

From the perspective of a DFA, authorities must ensure that reforms they undertake to mobilize domestic revenue are inclusive and sustainable development friendly. This implies considering the fiscal reforms' distributional impact or incentives on other aspects of sustainable development. A relevant example for Kazakhstan would be considering using fiscal policy toward public health priorities (Box 3). This would require a more in-depth analysis to explore options for establishing a sin tax to mobilize new financial resources for specific spending objectives, such as increasing health expenditure or a specific health program.

Social Spending

The composition of spending can be as important as the volume of public resources available, and redistributive spending can help rebalance regressive features in the tax system. Progressive taxation, well-targeted transfers and quality expenditure to benefit the poor have the potential to efficiently perform redistribution. Like taxes, social expenditures can reduce inequality.[10]

The total amount of social spending[11] decreased from $20,259 million in 2015 to $17,633 million in 2018.

---

[10] The experience of developed countries shows that sound fiscal policies can play an essential role in mitigating inequalities and also can foster sustainable growth. The dynamics of inequality are strongly influenced by management of public wealth, regulation of financial markets, labor laws and fiscal policies such as efforts to prevent tax evasion (Alvaredo et al., 2018).

[11] Social spending here includes public spending on health, education, and social protection, as provided in

Figure 12. Composition of Social Expenditure

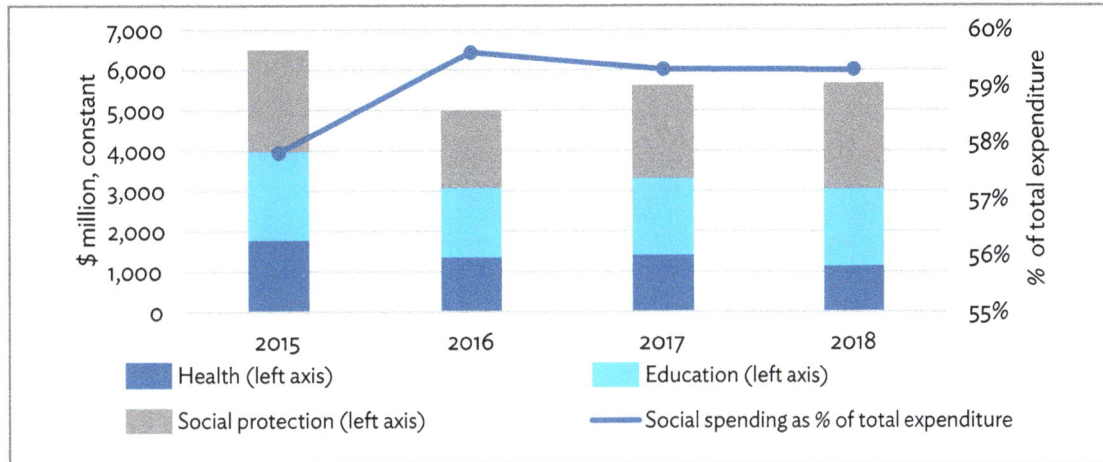

Source: Ministry of Finance of the Republic of Kazakhstan (State budget expenditures).

Despite this decrease the share of social spending in the state budget slightly increased to an average of 59% of total expenditure for the period 2015–2018 (Figure 12). The weight of spending on social protection gradually increased toward representing close to half of the social budget, to the detriment of mostly health related public spending.

Social safety nets such as unemployment benefits and social pensions can improve the resilience of households to economic shocks and, in this way, help to lift the most vulnerable individuals out of poverty (World Bank, 2018). Social protection policies in Kazakhstan include both social insurance programs (e.g., pensions and unemployment benefits) and social assistance. Coverage of social assistance is generally pro-poor and contributes to lowering income poverty, especially for persons with disabilities and those unable to work. Almost half of households in the bottom income quintile receive a social transfer for children, compared with one in five in the top three income quintiles.[12] However, a large share of low-income households does not receive the transfers they are entitled to. Overall, the level of benefits targeting children in low-income families is too low.[13]

As a result, the redistributive impact of Kazakhstan's fiscal system remains limited. The tax and transfer policies are estimated to reduce inequality by 7% in Kazakhstan, compared to 29% in OECD countries (OECD, 2016). The income support system currently plays a minor role in lowering inequality. The fall in inequality during the 2000s can be largely attributed to the evolution of market incomes, as the creation of salaried jobs accelerated, absorbing unemployment, and wage policy sustained widely distributed growth in incomes (footnote 13).

Improving the redistributive impact of its fiscal system, including NFRK transfers, requires revenue authorities to monitor the impact of their tax models on income distribution and other aspects of sustainable development, and incorporating this into the monitoring systems for national development

government data.

[12] B. Babajanian, J. Hagen-Zanker, and H. Salomon. 2015. 2015. *Analysis of Social Transfers for Children and their Families in Kazakhstan*. UNICEF.

[13] L. Carraro, J. Rogers, S. Rijicova. 2017. *Technical Support to Improve Design of Targeted Cash Transfer Program to be More Responsive to the Needs of Families with Children*. UNICEF.

plans. The UNU-WIDER and Tulane University's Commitment to Equity initiative have developed fiscal incidence models that are in the public domain and can be used to estimate the impact of fiscal policy on poverty and inequality in Kazakhstan. As a next step, Kazakhstan may want to consider establishing explicit equity targets for its revenue policy, alongside the more common revenue raising targets. Such equity targets may be useful to address the country's persistent regional inequalities, for instance.

Table 6. Comparison of Health and Education Expenditure with Regional Peers

	Current Health Expenditure (% of GDP)			Current Health Expenditure Per Capita (current $)			Adjusted Savings: Education Expenditure (% of GNI)		
	2005	2010	2016	2005	2010	2016	2005	2010	2016
Azerbaijan	7.4	4.9	6.9	114.8	287.7	268.2	3.3	2.9	3.0
Georgia	8.3	9.5	8.4	118.7	262.5	308.0	2.6	1.9	1.8
Kazakhstan	3.9	2.7	3.5	143.2	246.2	262.0	2.3	3.1	3.2
Kyrgyz Republic	7.5	7.0	6.6	36.1	61.5	72.9	4.8	5.8	5.7
Uzbekistan	5.0	5.4	6.3	27.2	72.3	135.1	9.4	9.4	9.4
Upper middle income	*5.3*	*5.6*	*5.9*	*165.2*	*356.3*	*454.8*	*N/A*	*N/A*	*N/A*
Lower middle income	*3.9*	*3.7*	*4.0*	*34.9*	*62.2*	*79.4*	*3.1*	*3.0*	*3.1*
Europe & Central Asia (excluding high income)	*5.2*	*5.2*	*5.2*	*230.1*	*417.2*	*371.2*	*3.5*	*3.7*	*3.8*
OECD members	*10.4*	*11.6*	*12.6*	*3262.1*	*4184.5*	*4667.6*	*4.3*	*4.6*	*4.5*

GDP = gross domestic product, GNI = gross national income, OECD = Organisation for Economic Co-operation and Development.
Source: World Bank, World Development Indicators.

The national budget, user fees, and voluntary health insurance are the main sources of financing for health care, although the share of out-of-pocket-pay are on the rise,[14] the 3.5% of GDP allocated to the health sector in 2016 is below Kazakhstan's neighboring countries and upper middle income countries where it averaged 5.9% of GDP in 2016 (Table 6). Implementation of the Compulsory Social Health Insurance is under way and will be fully operational from 2020[15] (UN CCA, 2019).

There is still room for improvement in increasing public spending in education and eliminating corruption. Public spending on education has greatly increased over the last decade; from 0.7% of GDP in 2000 to 4.1% in 2014, according to data from the Ministry of Education and Science of the Republic of Kazakhstan (MES). However, this level of expenditure remains below about 1 percentage point less on education than the average for emerging markets and developing economies (IMF; 2018b) and has since decreased to 3.3% of GDP in 2018.

Educational attainment has increased in the last decade, but further improvements in quality, relevance, and equity are required to allow young people's transition to productive employment (World Bank, 2018). This will likely require higher funding. Kazakhstan's spending per pupil (at 11.7% of GDP per capita) is less than half that in top Programme for International Student Assessment (PISA)–performing countries,

---

[14] World Health Organization Global Health Expenditure Database. Accessed 18 November 2019.

[15] http://dsm.gov.kz/ru/kategorii/o-vnedrenii-obyazatelnogo-socialnogo-medicinskogo-strahovaniya.

Figure 13. Evolution of the Share of Social Spending

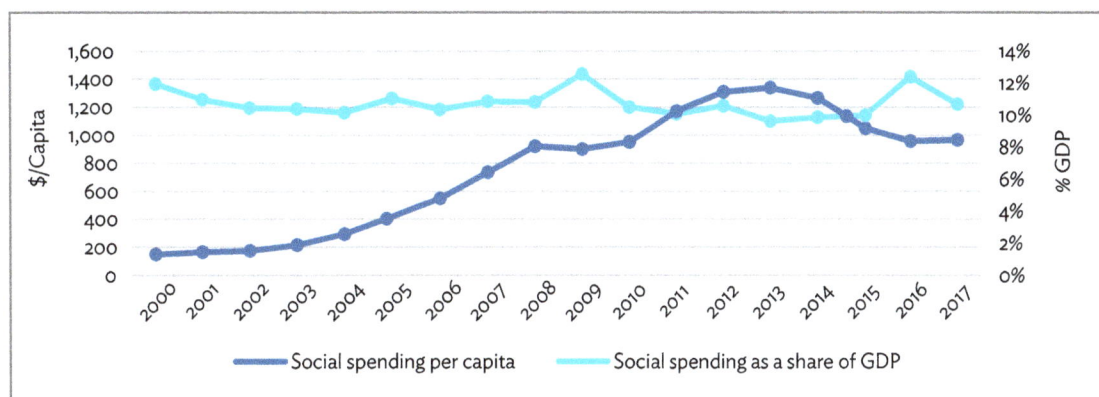

GDP = gross domestic product.
Source: ADB. 2019. Key Indicators for Asia and the Pacific. Manila. https://www.adb.org/publications/key-indicators-asia-and-pacific-2019.

Figure 14. Public Spending on Subsidies and Social Benefits

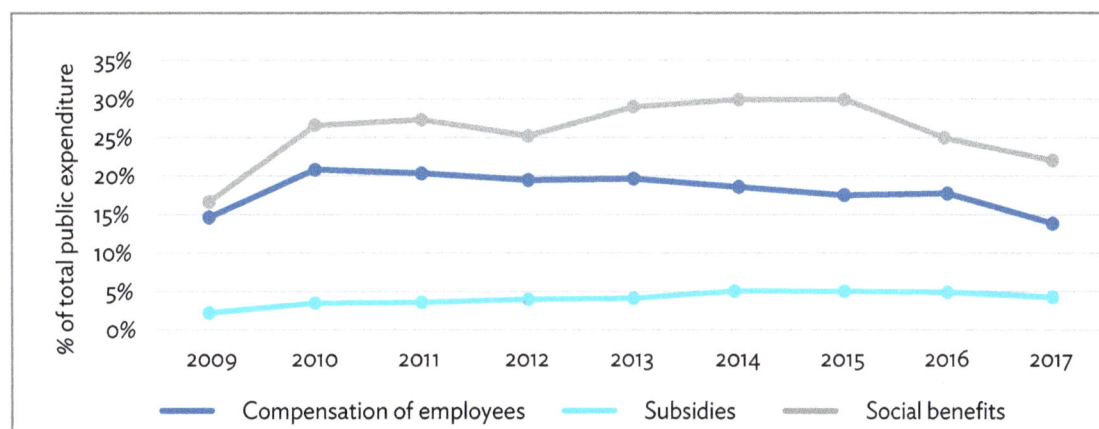

Source: ADB. 2019. Key Indicators for Asia and the Pacific. Manila. https://www.adb.org/publications/key-indicators-asia-and-pacific-2019

such as Estonia, Japan, Poland, and Switzerland. In addition, despite recent efforts, education continues to be considered as highly corrupt (Bertelsmann stiftung transformation Index, 2014), with corruption cases in the education system making up 16% of the overall number of corruption crimes in Kazakhstan (OECD, 2016).

While social expenditure has maintained its share of GDP during the past decade, there is a notable decline in the amount of the available public spending per capita. During Kazakhstan's strong economic growth years, available social spending per citizen increased tenfold from about $147 per capita in 2000 to $1,334 in 2013. By 2017 it had decreased to $963 per capita (Figure 13).

This points to a second important finding from this DFA, which is that the drop in available government revenue from 2014 onward translated into a significant reduction of the authorities' fiscal space[16] to raise citizens' living standards and strengthen human capital. The latter being a critical pillar for realizing the country's ambitious development vision. Indeed, expenditure on education and health systems that cover a wide range of the population may bring about better employment prospects, wider participation in the political process, and increased well-being, and so foster equality of opportunities (OECD, 2008). Additional revenues are needed to support consolidation, additional investment, and social outlays.

The decrease in social spending per capita occurred in the years where the discretionary transfers from the NFRK increased significantly to counter the impact of the low resource prices on government revenue. This indicates that human capital strengthening through investing in education, health, and social protection may not be a priority for using NFRK reserves.

Considering the projected contained economic growth and the structurally low oil prices government revenue growth is likely to remain subdued for the near future. This requires tapping into alternative sources of finance, such as debt financing and aligning private financial resources to maintain appropriate levels of investment in human capital. In her speech at the Astana Economic Forum in 2019, Christine Lagarde noted Kazakhstan's "fiscal policy should balance debt concerns with critical initiatives in health, education, and infrastructure".[17] For instance, public spending on education needs to be raised and improved to better align education and workers' skills with private sector needs (OECD, 2016).

To address the funding gap in health and education expenditure authorities are adapting a new "capitation" approach to provide funding to service providers on a per capita basis and to streamline health and education outlays, while increasing flexibility and service quality through expanded public–private partnerships (PPPs) and outsourcing (IMF, 2018).[18]

The Kazakhstan government faces a trade-off between lowering the non-oil deficit, to comply with the newly adopted fiscal rules, versus maintaining minimum levels of social spending to underpin living standards and social peace. The short-term discretionary financing solution adopted by the government so far, which consisted of additional targeted transfers from the NFRK, is now limited by the risks it poses on the NFRK's long–term sustainability. This requires addressing a complex balance of inter-generational equity while addressing pressing, immediate investment needs.

A possible way forward to ease the pressure on the state budget is by reducing harmful and ineffective subsidies. According to ADB data the share of subsidies in total government expenses rose from 2.1% in 2009 to 4.2% in 2017 for Kazakhstan. A large majority of public spending for agriculture still goes to subsidies. Kazakhstan also subsidizes the use and production of fossil fuels, such as coal, gas, and oil, as well as electricity, which are consumed directly by end users or as inputs to electricity generation. It is among the 15 countries with the highest subsidies in the world but is number one in subsidizing coal. Although energy subsidies aim to help the poor, in fact they benefit the highest income households

[16] Fiscal space: The World Bank's 2019 World Development Report on the future of work [9] suggests ways governments increase fiscal space in order to prepare for the future of work through investments in human capital and social protection.

[17] Lagarde, C. 2019. Finding a Path to the Higher Plain of Inclusive Growth. Astana Economic Forum – Nur-Sultan, Kazakhstan. International Monetary Fund.16 May. https://www.imf.org/en/News/Articles/2019/05/15/sp051619-lagarde-Kazakhstan-finding-a-path-to-the-higher-plain-of-inclusive-growth

[18] International Monetary Fund. 2018. Kazakhstan: Staff Concluding Statement of the 2018 Article IV Mission. 28 June. https://www.imf.org/en/News/Articles/2018/06/28/ms062818-kazakhstan-staff-concluding-statement-of-the-2018-article-iv-mission

more. Other subsidies include subsidized lending support to SMEs and households, which sometimes come from the NBK or from the pension fund, instead of the budget, undermining oversight and fiscal transparency (IMF, 2019).

The government undertook some reform of energy subsidies: most of the direct support for electricity and heat consumers was eliminated, while the government still provides indirect support by maintaining electricity and heat tariffs at low rates.[19] From a developmental perspective, it matters that the resources that are freed-up from subsidy reductions benefit the most vulnerable. This may not only be achieved through safety nets but also e.g, in ensuring infrastructure development or service delivery is improved for these communities.

State-Owned Enterprises

State companies and conglomerates dominate the business landscape in Kazakhstan. According to the OECD's Index of State Control, Kazakhstan has a greater presence of state-owned enterprises (SOEs) in the economy than any OECD member and most large non-OECD economies, including Brazil and the People's Republic of China (PRC). Accurate estimates of the share state entities represent in the country's GDP are hard to come by and vary according to the source. While public ownership has fallen compared to the Soviet era, OECD (2016) estimates the assets of the more than 750 national and municipal corporatized SOEs in operation still account for some 30% to 40% of GDP. According to government estimations based on the gross value-added (GVA) of the state sector to GDP,[20] state entities represented 17.3% at the end of 2017, compared to 21.1% in 2014.

Economies of scale or natural monopolies may justify the choice of SOEs above alternatives to provide public services or channel public investment. Such decisions need to be informed by objective assessments of the rationale for existing state ownership, considering the costs, benefits, and risks of state ownership, whether SOEs have clearly articulated objectives, and whether there are more-efficient means to achieve any noncommercial policy objectives.

Three public holding structures—Samruk-Kazyna, KazAgro, and Baiterek Holdings, along with their more than 600 subsidiaries—dominate the economy, controlling energy, transport, utilities, SME financing, and agriculture finance and product development. These public holding structures and SOEs dominate in sectors and market segments that, in other countries, are typically open to private participation, such as oil and gas production, electricity, transport, and telecoms.

Kazakhstan's large reliance on SOEs and corporatized former state enterprise has implications for governance, private sector development and fiscal risks:

- **Governance:** Government is heavily represented in the governance structures of major holding companies, with high-level officials assigned to serve as board members and heads. Good practice to strengthen government ownership policy includes centralized and depoliticized management of state shareholdings, selection of competent management and supervisory board members, and establishing supporting legal and regulatory frameworks.

- **Private sector** development: The pervasiveness of SOEs and their subsidiaries across all economic sectors severely undermines the level playing field for private competitors and investors. This contrast starkly with the government's strategic long-term development aims which rely on the existence of a

---

[19] Kazakhstan Environmental Performance Review, UNECE, 2019

[20] This method is defined by the OECD as the most preferable, as it reflects objective state participation in the economy, which allows analyzing this participation in various sectors of the economy.

thriving, diversified private sector. Analysis from the IMF, OECD, the World Bank and other external observers, such as the World Economic Forum, concur that Kazakhstan's large quasi-state sector constitutes a binding constraint to sustainably develop Kazakhstan's private sector.

- **Fiscal risks**: Contingent liabilities from PPPs and SOEs, if not duly incorporated in governments' balance sheets, may increase the fiscal risk to which the government is exposed. In the case of Kazakhstan, the government's strategy to prefer domestic borrowing to avoid currency risks, contradicts with the SOE's foreign borrowing practices. The IMF recommends efforts to strengthen fiscal transparency and risk management, including monitoring of SOEs and PPPs.

Given the limited fiscal space and the ensuing reduction in public investment, it is crucial to proceed with SOE reform and further privatization (IMF, 2018b). The government has advanced an ambitious privatization program as its top priority. As part of its ambition to reduce the government's share in the economy to 15% by 2020 and the share of SOE assets as a share of GDP to 30% by 2022 to Kazakhstan aims to sell more than 700 companies by 2020, with assets such as the national oil and mining companies available to foreign investors.

Privatization of SOEs promises greater productivity and efficiency and positive impact on public finances by reducing the implied costs of quasi-fiscal operations and transfers. More importantly more rapid progress is required on blue-chip initial public offerings in oil and gas, telecoms, aviation, energy, and railways to level the playing field for international investors and developing the domestic private sector.

While privatization processes are transparent, the implementation of the privatization plan is subject to challenges. Smooth privatization and development of a competitive private sector are also complicated by a non-transparent regulatory environment. Interest by local and foreign investors in purchasing privatized assets or in competing in markets dominated by large state or private firms may be reduced because of (sometimes non-transparent) regulatory burdens and price controls, including, for example, in the energy distribution networks and in telecommunications (OECD, 2016). While the commitments to privatization seem sincere, avoiding that privatization does not simply transfer rents to a small set of elites requires developing and sharing a vision for its plans in each subsector or major market in the economy (World Bank, 2018).

Public–Private Partnerships

Presently, Kazakhstan gained considerable experience in the implementation of PPP projects in various sectors, especially in the field of industrial infrastructure, innovation, transport, and social and public services (Gabdullina, 2012). There are special PPP laws and concession laws in place in Kazakhstan and as of July 2019, more than 500 PPP agreements have been concluded in Kazakhstan to the amount of T1.29 trillion ($3.34 billion)[21] (Figure 15). Nine of the projects were national and the rest were local. According to the government an additional 620 PPP projects worth T1.89 trillion ($4.91 billion) are under development.[22] Most the projects fall under education, health care, housing and communal services, culture, and sports. PPPs may thus provide an alternative to using scarce budget funding for the provision of health and education services.

Kazakhstan's developed regulatory and institutional framework for PPPs reflects the government's commitment to PPPs as a procurement modality. In 2015, a new PPP law was introduced to enhance

---

[21] PPP Knowledge Lab. https://pppknowledgelab.org/countries/kazakhstan

[22] Zhussupova, D. 2019. Public-private partnerships contracts worth $3 billion concluded in first half of 2019. *The Astana Times.* 25 July. https://astanatimes.com/2019/07/public-private-partnerships-contracts-worth-3-billion-concluded-in-first-half-of-2019/

Figure 15. Largest Public–Private Partnership Projects in Kazakhstan

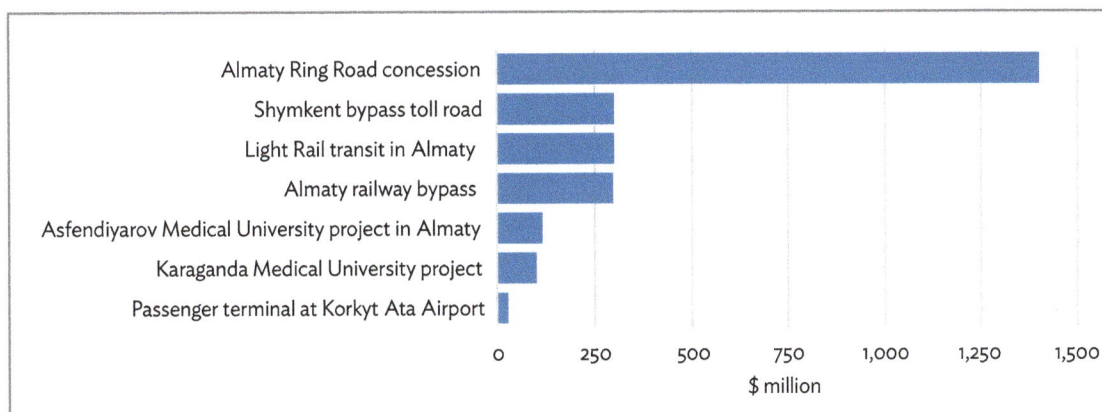

Source: Economist Intelligence Unit, Infrascope.

existing Concession Laws and provide guidance with PPP planning and project implementation processes. Under the PPP law, a specialized PPP unit, the Public–Private Partnership Centre under the MNE, was established to facilitate and promote PPP projects. The independent Kazakhstan Project Preparation Fund—a $6.3 million joint venture between the JSC Kazakhstan Public–Private Partnership Centre and JSC National Holding Baiterek—aims to promote infrastructure development through the provision of services, including structuring and implementation support and assistance with developing relevant documentation. The PPP Center has enabled to synthesize the accumulated experience gained by Kazakhstan in pursuing concession-based projects. It has built certain human, expertise, and institutional bases regarding PPP development (Chikanayev, 2012). City governments of Oskemen and Karaganda opened their own PPP centers to boost regional development.

Kazakhstan scores 59 out of 100 on the "infrascope index,"[23] which measures the

Figure 16. Enabling environment for PPP in infrastructure

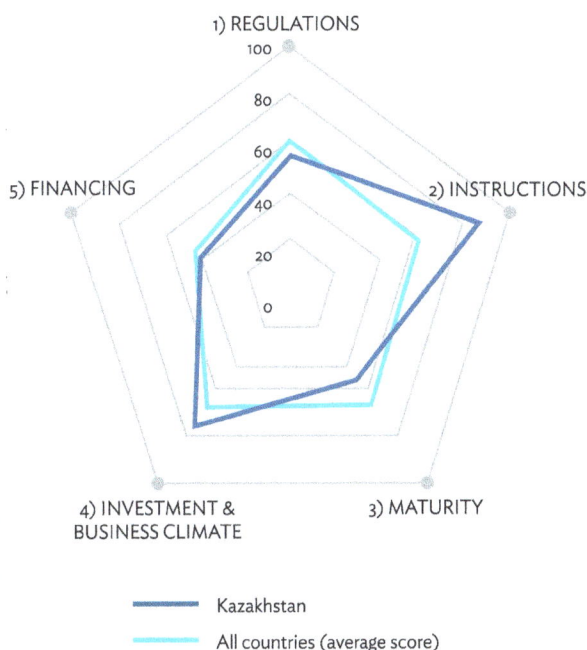

Kazakhstan — All countries (average score)

PPP = Public-private partnership
Source: Economist Intelligence Unit, Infrascope, 2019.

[23] The Infrascope index is a benchmarking tool that evaluates the capacity of countries to implement sustainable and efficient in key infrastructure sectors, principally transport, electricity, water, and solid waste management.

Figure 17. Evolution of Public Borrowing

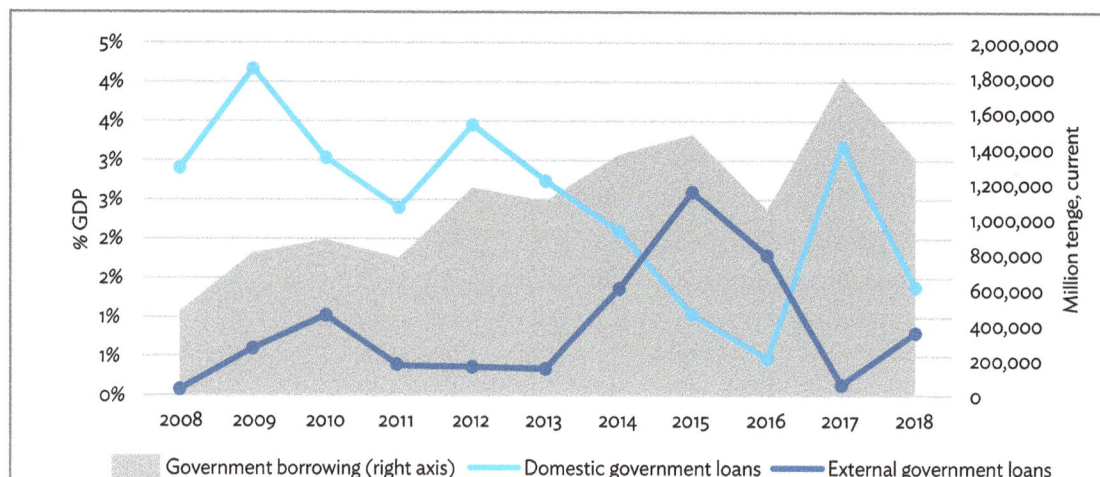

GDP = gross domestic product.
Source: Ministry of Finance.

enabling environment for PPPs in infrastructure (Figure 16). This compares favorably to the EMEA region's average score of 54 and places Kazakhstan in the category of "emerging" PPP environment, on the brink of passing to the "developed" PPP environment. Out of the 5 dimensions assessed Kazakhstan score best on "Institutions" with a high score of 85 out of 100, followed by the business and investment environment scoring 72 out of 100. Further progress is required on the dimensions of maturity (48 out of 100) and Financing (42 out of 100).

The World Bank (2018) notes that despite considerable progress establishing this enabling environment for the delivery of public infrastructure and services through PPPs, activities have been limited. For example, while there are more than 100 projects in the government's Master PPP Pipeline, implementation has not followed suit. This concurs with the EIU's 2019 Infrascope ranking of Kazakhstan, which ranks the country low on the "PPP Maturity" dimension.[24] While Kazakhstan scores in the top tier for political will to pursue PPPs, the low maturity score indicates a mismatch between intention and execution, as well as possible systemic impediments, including corruption perception, that are limiting private appetite for infrastructure PPPs.

The major risks and challenges associated with PPP projects in infrastructure in Kazakhstan include poor quality project selection and project preparation at the local (municipal) level; a lack of transparency regarding the bid process and decision-making; processes for dealing with change management, including contract variations, the treatment of contingent liabilities, renegotiation mechanisms, including penalties and compensation mechanisms; public disclosure requirements; and independent oversight. There is also inadequate long-term financing for PPP projects in local currency, including through capital markets that are not developed enough to support infrastructure financing. The World Bank's Infrastructure Sector Assessment (InfraSAP) may ease some of the capacity constraints by identifying opportunities to maximize finance for priority investments and the sequenced actions needed to unlock those opportunities.

---

[24] This dimension covers the extent to which countries and subnational governments have experience in delivering PPPs.

Assessing the contribution of PPPs to progress against Kazakhstan's strategic development programs is difficult, since there are few reliable, up-to-date data sources that comprehensively cover PPP projects across most sectors of the economy on a consistently measured basis.

Public Borrowing

Borrowing enables government to make investments that would otherwise take longer to fund, working on the basis that greater public investment stimulates development that will generate returns that can be used to repay debts. Maintaining public debt sustainability requires assessing the long-term prospects for increased revenue mobilization and ask whether their tax and financing systems can provide the resources needed to support the public investments they need to yield the sustainable development results they are striving toward.

Government borrowing does not represent a major source of development finance for Kazakhstan. While absolute amounts of annual borrowing are increasing year on year, their relative size to GDP decreased from a peak of 4.8% of GDP in 2009 to 2.2% in 2018. Except for the period of economic slowdown during 2014-20 public borrowing was predominantly domestic (Figure 18).

Figure 18. General Government Gross Debt   Figure 19. Total External Debt Stocks
                                                                              (by debtor type)

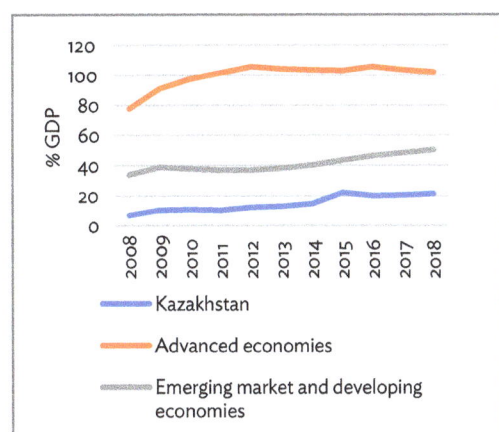

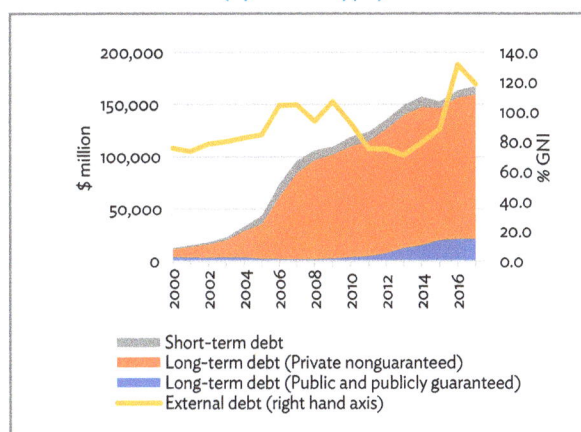

GDP = gross domestic product, GNI = gross national income.
Source: International Monetary Fund.

As a result, the share of general government gross debt to GDP, which stood at 21% in 2018 is low compared to other emerging market and developing economies, where debt to GDP represented 50.6% (and Figure 19). External observers consider Kazakhstan's public debt to be manageable, which implies the possibility to increase the use of debt financing toward addressing infrastructure needs. However, this margin for using debt financing depends on the evolution of the reserve assets of the NFRK. The impetus to restore fiscal sustainability and provide a strong signal to financial markets of the government's strict adherence to the new fiscal rules may limit the use of additional debt financing in coming years to frontload infrastructure investments.

Kazakhstan's public and publicly guaranteed external debt equivalent to 21% of GDP in 2018 is low compared to debt levels of other UMICs. Large currency depreciations in recent years have underscored Kazakhstan's exposure to foreign currency-denominated debt and may explain the government's

Figure 20. Composition of External Debt in Kazakhstan and Upper Middle-Income Countries

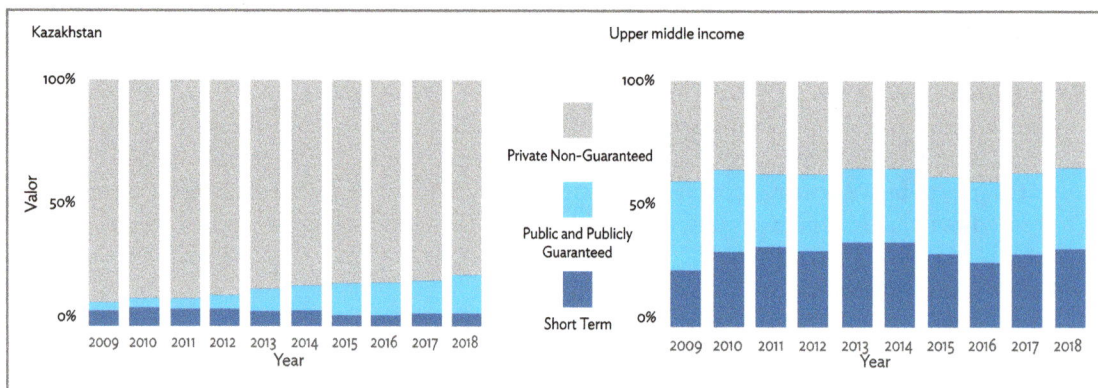

Source: World Bank. Debt Data. http://datatopics.worldbank.org/debt/

Table 7. Outstanding Bond Issues

Currency	Outstanding bond issues	Cumulative volume
sovereign		
KZT	160	10,523,945,628,700
USD	4	6,500,000,000
EUR	4	2,200,000,000
municipal		
KZT	46	254,989,280,000
corporate		
KZT	277	11,698,309,000,990
USD	34	16,709,820,000
RUB	13	77,000,000,000
CHF	2	435,000,000

CHF = Swiss franc, EUR = euro, KZT = Kazakhstan tenge, RUB = Russian ruble, USD = United States dollar.
Source: Cbonds. http://cbonds.com/countries/Kazakhstan_bond

predominant use of domestic currency denominated debt. This predominance of using domestic debt in a context of shallow domestic credit markets need to be weighed of against the risk of crowding out access to credit by the private sector.

The debt sustainability assessment changes when Kazakhstan's corporate debt, which is mainly SOE debt and therefore a contingent liability for the government, is included as part of total public sector

Figure 21. Sectoral Allocation of Public Sector External Debt Position, 2018

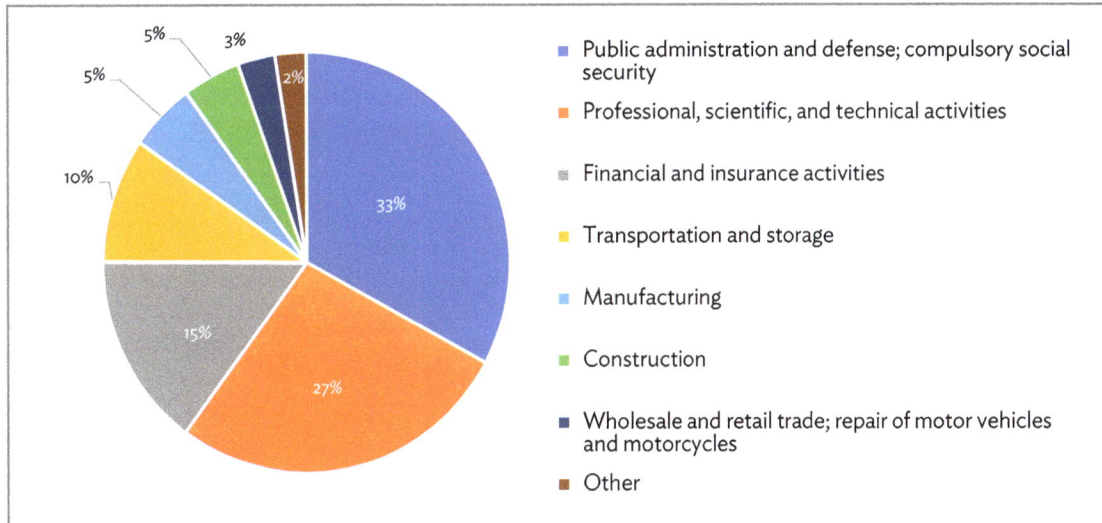

Source: Ministry of Finance, Republic of Kazakhstan.

debt. This alternative, more realistic, perspective suggests greater concern over fiscal sustainability. Sound public sector debt management would benefit from integrating SOE debt within the public debt management strategy toward developing an integrated management of public assets and liabilities and comprehensive and transparent oversight of public sector fiscal policy (World Bank, 2017). This approach would allow identifying contradictions between the government's debt strategy and the SOE debt profiles. The magnitude of such contradictions may be significant. In Kazakhstan, private non-guaranteed debt largely outweighs public and publicly guaranteed debt (Figure 20). Considering the extensive role of state enterprises and equity holdings in "private" companies most private non-guaranteed debt has de facto (as opposed to de jure) guarantees of subsidies/bail-outs behind them.

For governments, bond markets provide a tool for raising the types of funding needed to support SDGs and for managing and helping to create an appropriate macroenvironment for long-term financing. Local currency bond markets can support diversifying financial intermediary channels and mitigate the impacts of financial crises. They also have the potential to help mobilize the country's savings to meet its infrastructure investment needs. According to CBOND, Kazakhstan has the equivalent of $36 billion sovereign bonds and $48 billion corporate bonds outstanding. Two-thirds of its outstanding bonds are tenge denominated (Table 7).

Public sector external debt stock is allocated predominantly to public administration and the tertiary sector. Management consultancies and financial services represented 42% of total debt allocation, whereas the agriculture, manufacturing, and construction sectors together represented little more than 10%. As such, public debt does not seem to be geared toward financing productive investments.

Development Partners and International Financial Institutions

Kazakhstan, being an UMIC, perceives little to no ODA. Total ODA flows since 2008 amounted $814 million. In 2018 only $3 million was reported to the OECD DAC.

Besides ODA, development partners may support Kazakhstan's development priorities through nonconcessional loans, providing technical assistance, analytical capacity and crowding in private sector finance. These nonconcessional aid modalities typically proceed from IFIs. They are recorded under the concept of other official flows (OOF)[25] in the OECD Creditor Reporting System (CRS). In 2016, OOF to Kazakhstan peaked at 1.4% of GDP, equivalent to $1.9 billion (Figure 22). While relatively small, these loans pursue sustainable developmental objectives and hence may be used strategically to catalyze support for investment in niche areas such as climate finance and global and regional public goods across the region.

Several major IFIs are present in Kazakhstan, including the World Bank, the Asian Development Bank (ADB), the European Bank for Reconstruction and Development (EBRD), and the International Finance Cooperation (IFC). Beyond their financial contributions IFIs support attracting private sector investment, expand their knowledge work, and introduce technological innovations. Table 8 provides an overview of the total amount of resources development partners provided to Kazakhstan through grants and loans since 1994.

Development partners cite the government's capacity constraints and difficulties to effectively engage with the appropriate government counterparts as undermine realizing their full development contributions to the country. The implementation of complex projects involving different line ministries may be delayed or not proceed at all due to coordination issues.

To date, EBRD's current investment portfolio represents €2,642 million, spread across 126 projects. Of this portfolio, 65% is targeted at sustainable infrastructure, 31% to industry, commerce, and agribusiness and the remainder to financial institutions. One recent EBRD project aims to support local currency lending to the micro, small, and medium-sized enterprises (MSME) sector in Kazakhstan by providing long-term financing to the regions outside the cities of Nur-Sultan and Almaty.

Examples of recent ADB projects include strengthening access to finance for MSME, especially those located in rural areas and led by women, and modernizing transport infrastructure along the Aktobe-Makat and Zhetybai-Zhanaozen roads. ADB is supporting PPPs as well as private sector projects in renewable energy, transport, health, and affordable housing. ADB also provided countercyclical support facilities amounting to $1 billion in 2015, which helped the country mitigate negative impacts from the economic downturn due to the decline of commodity prices. ADB also promotes domestic bond markets as an alternative to bank lending. These local currency funding solutions mitigate currency risks and channel savings from institutional investors toward financing development outcomes.

Thus, based on the little detailed project information available the sectoral priorities of the IFIs are more in tune with Kazakhstan's national development priorities than the international commercial finance flows, which have tended to concentrate in resource-related activities (Figure 23). It would be relevant to recompose the full picture of IFI engagement in the country and how they align with SDG priorities as well as contribute to strengthening SDG financing mechanisms in Kazakhstan.

---

[25] OOFs are defined as official sector transactions that do not meet ODA criteria. OOFs include grants to developing countries for representational or essentially commercial purposes; official bilateral transactions intended to promote development, but having a grant element of less than 25%; and, official bilateral transactions, whatever their grant element, that are primarily export-facilitating in purpose. This category includes: export credits extended directly to an aid recipient by an official agency or institution (official direct export credits); the net acquisition by governments and central monetary institutions of securities issued by multilateral development banks at market terms; subsidies (grants) to the private sector to soften its credits to developing countries; and, funds in support of private investment.

Figure 22. Official Development Aid and Other Official Flows to Kazakhstan

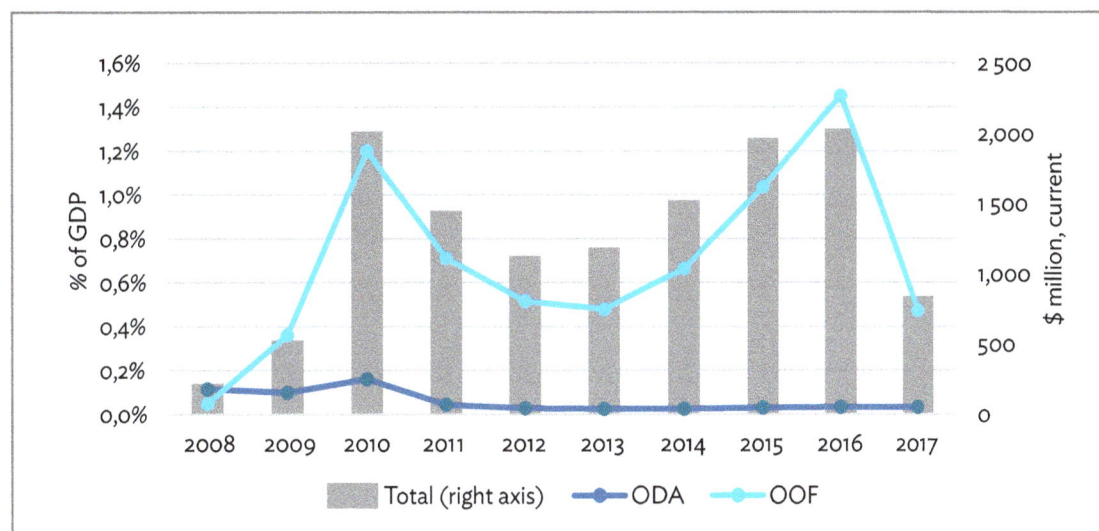

GDP = gross domestic prroduct, ODA = official development assistance, OOF = other official flows.
Source: Organisation for Economic Co-operation and Development. Common Reporting Standard, 2019.

Table 8. Kazakhstan Government External Borrowing and Grants from 1994–2019

Development partner	Grants	Loans
ADB	$47.1 million (94 projects)	$4.6 billion (28 projects)
EBRD	*Pending MNE data*	€7.5 billion (246 projects)
EU	€140 million (300 projects)	Does not provide loans
IsDB	$3.1 million	$2 billion (67 projects)
OECD	*Pending MNE data*	*Pending MNE data*
UNDP	$200 million (200 projects)	Does not provide loans
World Bank	*Pending MNE data*	$8.1 billion (46 projects)

ADB = Asian Development Bank, EBRD = European Bank for Reconstruction and Development, EU = European Union, IsDB = Islamic Development Bank, MNE = Ministry of National Economy, OECD = Organisation for Economic Co-operation and Development, UNDP = United Nations Development Programme.
Source: Compilation provided by the Kazakhstan.

It is hard to come by the exact amount and type of support provided by the multiple development partners still present in the country. This complicates maximizing their impact to the country's development outcomes. Beyond knowing their respective financial contributions and strategic priorities, it would be important to map their respective government counterparts for different projects. This information should ideally be centralized at the MNE, responsible for medium-term fiscal planning. This would allow for better coordination and alignment with Kazakhstan's sectoral development priorities. In parallel, development partners should set up a regular, more formal coordination mechanism to share information on their respective investment priorities and modalities as well as regional approaches.

Beyond providing financing, which in Kazakhstan remains small compared to total available development finance, development partners can play a critical role in strengthening the country's institutional and regulatory environment — the latter being identified as a binding constraint by recent OECD and the World Bank diagnostic analysis. Strengthening institutional capacity is critical to enable Kazakhstan implement the proposed reforms toward transitioning to a market-led, sustainable development model.

They can contribute their analytical capacity and technical expertise to crowd-in critical private investments through tailored, innovative financing approaches. For example, they might decide to cover partial project costs through viability gap funding for projects that are economically but not financially viable because they lack the ability to raise the requisite revenues to cover project costs. IFIs may also provide guarantees to cover risks that the private partner is not ready to take on, such as foreign exchange risks, debt repayment and minimum revenue or demand.

Examples of such analytical contributions to the country's long-term strategic thinking is the World Bank's recent Country Private Sector Diagnostic (CPSD), which identified opportunities for action to spur private sector-led growth in Kazakhstan. Development partner support may also be particularly relevant to build the government's capacity to implement its PPP Strategy.

Another important strategic area of development finance to which multilateral development partners and IFIs can facilitate access through their support is facilitating access to climate related development finance.

Climate-Related Development Finance

The Ministry of Energy is a lead ministry for energy policies and governance and has been involved in a range of climate-related projects supported by international development partners. Many other ministries and government agencies have been engaged in climate actions, such as the Ministry of Agriculture and Ministry of Industry and Infrastructural Development.

Kazakhstan has adopted a range of legal and policy frameworks on addressing issues concerning climate change and a wider set of sustainable development agenda. These include the "Concept for Transition to a Green Economy," the "Law on Energy Saving and Energy Efficiency," and the "Law on Supporting the Use of Renewable Energy Sources," the "Law on the Adaptation to Climate Change and a Low-Carbon Strategy" that would relate to, for instance, green technology development, the Kazakh Emission Trading Scheme and policies to promote renewable energies.

Kazakhstan submitted its intended nationally determined contribution (INDC) in 2015 with the quantitative target to reduce greenhouse gas (GHG) emissions. It communicated both a conditional target (on additional international support) and an unconditional target: GHG reduction by 25% below 1990 levels by 2030 (conditional) and 15% below 1990 level by 2030 (unconditional). One handicap of Kazakhstan's INDC is that it does not mention the means of implementation to meet its targets, neither on finance, or on required capacity development.

Beyond reducing GHG emissions and transitioning toward greater use of renewable energy sources, the World Bank[26] identified Kazakhstan's management of its natural water resources to be of strategic relevance to both the country's and the region's economic development. The combined effects of climate variability, growing populations, rising incomes, and expanding cities will see demand for water rising exponentially, while supply becomes more erratic and uncertain. Water resources in the region are sensitive to climate variability, which poses significant challenges to the agriculture and energy sectors.

[26] World Bank. 2019. No More Business as Usual: Improving Water Usage in Central Asia. https://www.worldbank.

There is no accurate recording of the total amount of climate-related development finance to Kazakhstan. According to an OECD (2016b[27]) study on financing climate action in Kazakhstan about $346.7 million of climate-related development finance was committed during the biennium 2013–2014. Mitigation projects represented 91% of the total. The volume of climate-related development finance committed to Kazakhstan was slightly larger than the average amount in the Eastern Europe, the Caucasus and Central Asia (EECCA) countries ($303 million per year), while the country's GDP per capita PPP is the highest in the EECCA region.

A significantly large share of climate-related development finance is delivered through multilateral channels and vertical funds ($311 million per year, or 89.6% of total) in 2013 and 2014. Examples include the EBRD and the European Investment Bank (EIB), using nonconcessional loans, and the Climate Investment Funds (CIF) with concessional loans. The European Union as well as other bilateral donors have provided a significant amount of grant financing to, for instance, technical assistance.

The largest amount of climate-related development finance was committed to energy efficiency and renewable energy projects in the energy generation and supply sector, which aligns well with the country's national policies on promoting low-carbon energy development. Climate-related finance targeting the banking and financial sector mostly represents the extension of credit lines by multilateral development banks (e.g., the EIB) to local banks, aiming to help SMEs finance mainly renewable energy or energy efficiency measures on the demand side.

Untapped international sources and modalities of climate-related development finance provide a strategic opportunity for Kazakhstan to finance its transition away from reliance on finite hydrocarbon reserves toward improved management and use of renewables. According to Climate Bonds Initiatives,[28] investors with $45 trillion of assets under management have made public commitments to climate and responsible investments. The challenge resides in attracting a share of this potentially available international commercial finance. Developing green bonds can help them achieve their pledges in fixed income. The key difference between conventional and green bonds is the specified use of proceeds. Investors are increasingly focused on integrating environment, social and governance (ESG) factors into their investment processes. Green bonds meet these environmental objects.

Domestic public finance is critical for climate finance—both directly for adaptation funding and as a catalyst for carbon neutral or low-carbon private investments by the private sector. Domestic public financing mechanisms cofinance climate-related project supported by international sources. For instance, the Sovereign Wealth Fund *Samruk-Kazyna* has invested significantly in several projects on renewable energy, among others. There are also policy instruments to provide fiscal incentives toward scaling up renewable energy. A feed-in tariff scheme and tax exemption schemes have also been put in place (OECD, 2016)

However, the scale of budgetary expenditure on climate finance is unclear. To allow a more strategic use of domestic public resources toward financing Kazakhstan's environmentally sustainable socioeconomic development in line with its multiple strategic programs and plans requires identifying and tracking budget allocations that respond to climate change challenges. Undertaking a systematic qualitative and quantitative analysis of a country's public expenditures and how they relate to climate change, in the form of a CPEIR, could inform a more holistic and effective government approach toward mitigating and adapting to climate change. Through the realization of a CPEIR authorities could further explore the value of establishing a climate budget tagging system to monitor and manage its climate related expenditure year-on-year.

---

org/en/news/feature/2019/06/28/no-more-business-as-usual-improving-water-usage-in-central-asia

[27] OECD. 2016. Financing Climate Action in Kazakhstan. Paris. https://www.oecd.org/environment/outreach/Kazakhstan_Financing_Climate_Action.Nov2016.pdf

[28] The Climate Bonds Initiative. Investor Appetite. https://www.climatebonds.net/market/investor-appetite

DOMESTIC AND INTERNATIONAL PRIVATE FINANCE

The contribution of private finance[29] flows to a country's sustainable development outcomes is critical through both the investments and recurrent spending it supports. Commercial actors small and large are a key part of all advanced economies and how they create jobs, develop skills, treat the environment, drive innovation and stimulate growth affect the development paths that countries may ultimately follow.

The difficulty resides in the fact that governments can only indirectly influence the scope and magnitude of private investment in the country. Managing the trade-offs between attracting commercial investment, for example with incentives or relaxed regulations, while maximizing its sustainable development impact—the jobs created, skills developed, innovation spurred on, green growth generated and so on—is a challenge.

As a first step, understanding the scale and nature of private financing is critical for considering the role that different private actors can play and, from the perspective of government, what partnerships, policies and interventions are needed to realize those roles toward supporting sustainable development.

Domestic Commercial Investment

According to government data domestic commercial investment represents the major source of private "commercial" finance in Kazakhstan (Figure 23). Following the global economic crisis in 2008 domestic commercial investment marked a slight decline from 10.6% of GDP in 2008 to 8.1% of GDP in 2011. The crisis exposed a real estate bubble, which significantly affected the domestic banking sector through the high share of nonperforming loans. The latter translated into a drop in domestic credit to the private sector, which is only starting to show signs of recovery in 2019 (Figure 24). Despite the declining trend of available domestic credit, domestic commercial investment continuously increased as a share of GDP from 2011 onward up to a record 13.2% of GDP in 2018.

This omnipresence of the quasi-state sector across Kazakhstan's economy makes it difficult to distinguish the sector's contribution to commercial investment from the contribution of Kazakhstan's domestic private enterprise sector.

Therefore, the marked sustained increase in domestic commercial investment from 2015 onward are likely the countercyclical spending measures channeled through the quasi-state sector and the three major holdings, Samruk Kazyna, Baiterek, and Kazagro. This illustrates the difficulties encountered in identifying how the non-state related private sector is evolving and investing. This makes it very difficult for the government to develop effective policy solutions to underpin private sector development and diversification.

For a DFA it is critical to adequately interpret the composition and dynamics of domestic commercial investment. Therefore, building a more integrated public and private approach to financing SDGs may require improving the data on non-state owned domestic commercial investments.

Except for the multinational enterprises, most of the large domestic commercial companies in Kazakhstan are somehow state-related. About one-fourth of Kazakhstan's 8.6 million employees in 2016 worked in public establishments (state education, health, research, or administrative organizations) or in SOEs (World Bank, 2018). In the context of this DFA we can therefore assume that Kazakhstan's domestic private enterprise sector mostly consists of MSMEs.

---

[29] Private finance here refers to domestic commercial investment, foreign direct investment, portfolio investment, borrowing by the private sector and remittances.

Figure 23. Sectoral Allocation of Other Official Flows to Kazakhstan, 2009–2017

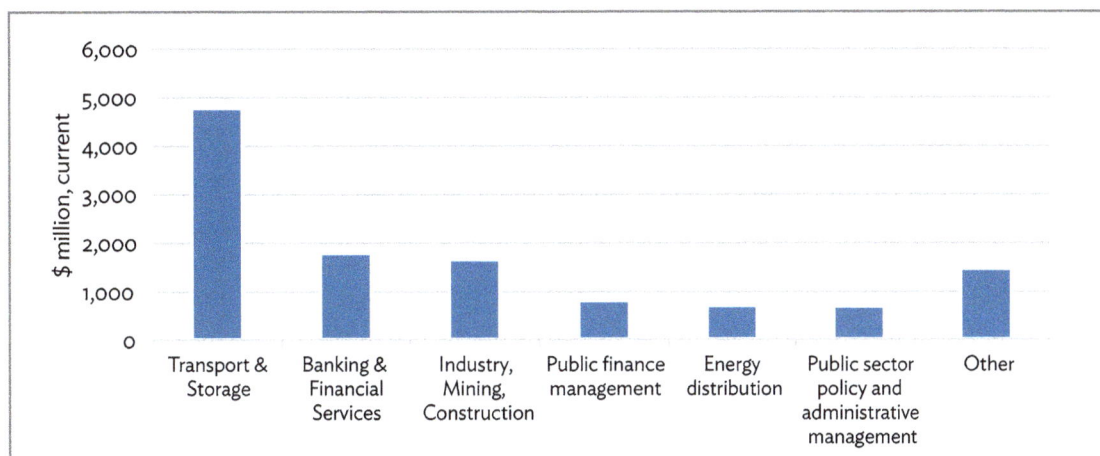

Source: Organisation for Economic Co-operation and Development, Common Reporting Standard.

Figure 24. Evolution of Private Finance in Kazakhstan

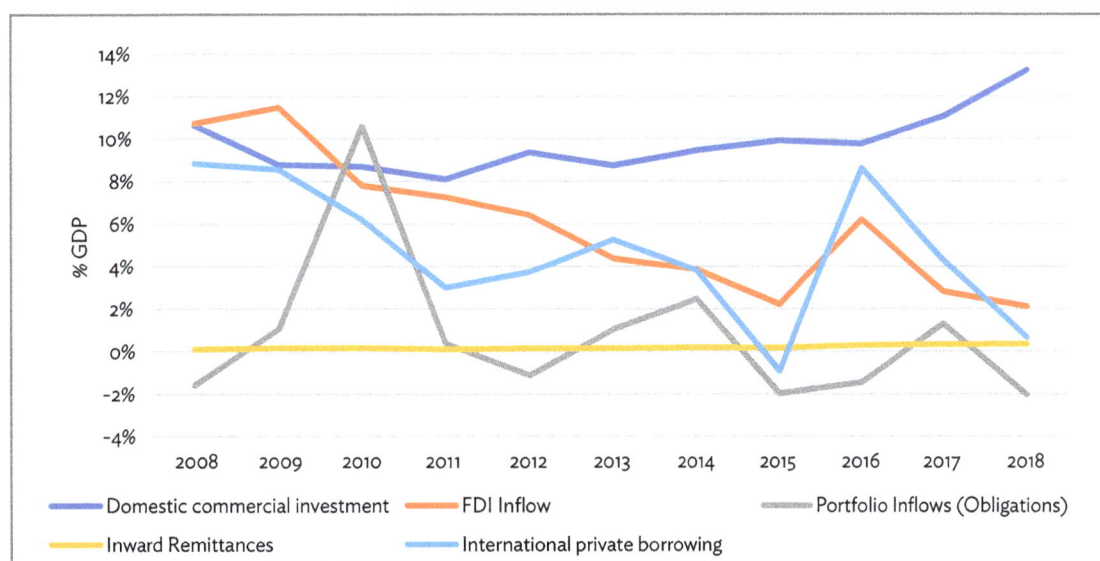

FDI = foreign direct investment.
GDP = gross domestic product
Sources: Ministry of finance of the Republic of Kazakhstan, National Bank of Kazakhstan, World Bank
Remittances Database and World Bank International Debt Statistics.

It is therefore worrisome that SMEs are particularly underdeveloped in Kazakhstan. The World Bank (2018) estimates that SMEs (including both private and public sector SMEs) account for 20% of GDP but just 28% of jobs. For comparison, in Saudi Arabia, SMEs account for 20% of GDP but 51% of jobs, and in the United Arab Emirates, they account for 30% of GDP but 86% of jobs. The number of SMEs increased by an average of 12%, employment by 10%, and GDP by 19% per annum between 2002 and 2013 (OECD; 2018). However, the SME population includes many very small firms (including those run by independent entrepreneurs). There is also a strong sector weighting of businesses toward the agriculture, wholesale and retail trade and much more limited numbers of SMEs in manufacturing. The World Bank concludes that the lack of dynamic small and mid-sized private companies, which tend to drive innovation globally, is a major constraint to the diversification and value-added of Kazakhstan's economy. SMEs in Kazakhstan are highly dependent on the banking sector to meet their financing needs.

Financial Sector Development

The lack of access to finance is a major constraint to the growth and diversification of domestic private enterprises in Kazakhstan. Although more than 90% of firms hold a checking or savings account, only 19% hold a bank loan or a credit line, well below other Eastern European and Central Asian countries (OECD; 2018). Furthermore, a large proportion of Kazakhstan businesses have had a recent loan request rejected (30%). This might be linked to the very low proportion of firms with audited financial statements (23%) and the high collateral requirements applied by local banks. Setting up a dedicated SME credit rating agency may be a response to these concerns.

The banking sector is largely domestically owned and relatively concentrated, with the largest five banks accounting for more than 75% of total banking assets. The banking sector remains saddled with weak underwriting and reporting standards, poor payment culture, related party and directed lending, opacity of ownership, and reliance on state support (IMF, 2019).

The banking sector has also been a source of considerable volatility in the economy. In 2005–2007, total credit grew at an average annual rate of nearly 60% in nominal terms (Figure 25), reaching 61% of GDP in 2007. Since 2007, however, credit growth to the private sector (relative to GDP) has declined, due in large part to the ongoing problem of legacy nonperforming loans (NPLs) following the banking crisis in 2007–2008 and Kazakhstan's real estate market collapse. The IMF projects private sector credit to resume, largely underpinned by consumer loans to households. Insufficient demand by creditworthy borrowers and limited availability of long-term funding are key constraints to a faster corporate credit growth toward actors and sectors of the economy that can drive sustainable, inclusive growth.

The pervasiveness of the quasi-state sector is also noticeable in the country's financial sector and the government's approach to expand credit to households and SOEs through subsidy programs. Funds have been sourced from international creditors, but also the NFRK and the state Unified Pension Fund (UPF) at attractive rates of return on capital and have been advanced at favorable rates to recipients. Activities of this quasi-public banking sector dwarf those of commercial banks. Their activities have included the economic stimulus program, lines of credit from international institutions, and allocation of UPF assets to commercial banks. This approach has on the one hand created fiscal costs and on the other distorted investment incentives for recipients. It also cannot address the fundamental shortage of credit to the economy (World Bank, 2017).

In 2018, the government inaugurated the Astana International Financial Center (AIFC) as a financial hub to hasten the development of local stock and bond markets as alternative sources of funds for firms and innovative financial products including Islamic finance banking and developing the fintech industry.

Figure 25. Evolution of Domestic Credit to the Private Sector

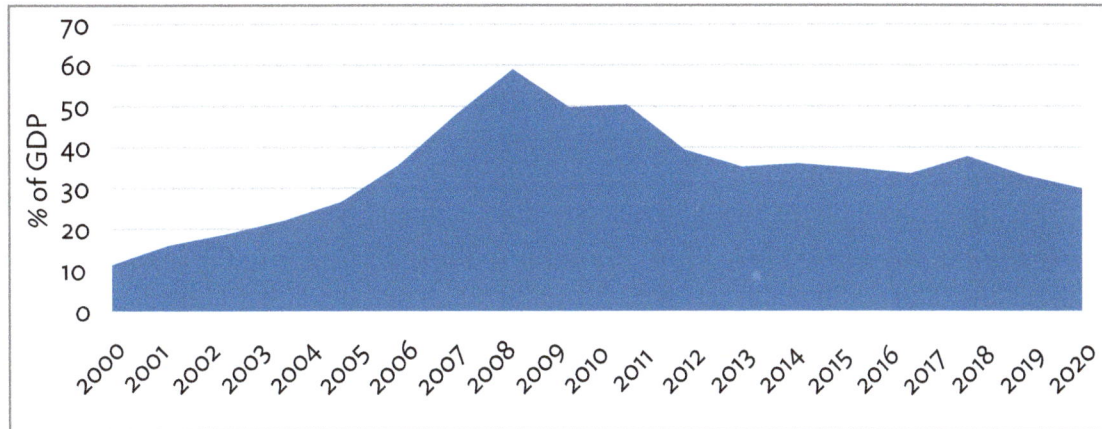

GDP = gross domestic product
Source: World bank, World Development Indicators.

Islamic Finance

Islamic finance[30] is a rapidly growing component of the financial sector in the world. According to Global Islamic finance report of 2017, the annual turnover of the Islamic finance market is estimated at $2.293 trillion, which is 1% of all world assets, and average growth rate of World Islamic finance is 13.9% between 2009–2017. Considering these trends Kazakhstan aims to become a regional hub for Islamic finance in and around Central Asia. According to Bello Danbatta, the Secretary General of the Islamic Financial Services Board (IFSB) Kazakhstan can be the potential hub for Islamic banking in and around Central Asia.[31]

The first Islamic bank in the region, Al Hilal, was established in 2010. Now, the domestic market of Islamic finance has evolved to represent two Islamic banks (Al Hilal Bank and Zaman Bank); Islamic leasing companies "Ijara" and Al-Saqr Finance; Islamic micro finance company "New Finance;" and Islamic insurance company "Takaful." among others.

Currently, Islamic finance accounts for less than 1% of the country's total banking assets. The aim is to increase this share to 3%-5% by 2025 with support of the AIFC[32] and IFIs such as ADB. Recently the AIFC management announced intent to issue *sukuk,* or Islamic bonds, for investment, infrastructure, and environmental projects by the end of the year. Unlike traditional bonds, *sukuk* does not imply a fixed income, since sharia prohibits interest.

---

[30] Islamic finance, also known as Islamic banking, complies with Islamic law, known as sharia, and includes such modes as mudarabah (profit-sharing and loss-bearing), wadiah (safekeeping), musharaka (joint venture), murabahah (cost-plus), and ijara (leasing). Sharia prohibits usury, or lending money and charging interest, while investments in businesses that provide goods or services considered contrary to Islamic principles such as pork and alcohol are also prohibited.

[31] Gadimova, N. 2019. In Muslim-Majority Kazakhstan, Islamic Banking Could Have Potential. The Caspian News. 26 July. https://caspiannews.com/news-detail/in-muslim-majority-kazakhstan-islamic-banking-could-have-potential-2019-7-26-27/

[32] https://aifc.kz/news/pri-podderzke-mezdunarodnogo-finansovogo-centra-astana-prezentovano-issledovanie-ob-islamskih-finansah-v-kazahstane

Financial Inclusion and Microfinance

Financial inclusion is a critical dimension to implementing the "leaving no one behind" dimension of the 2030 Agenda. Ensuring fair access to finance in remote regions or to disfavored segments of the population can support them developing economic livelihoods. Kazakhstan compares well against global peers on broad measures of financial inclusion. More than 59% of the population over age 15 has an account at a financial institution and 54% made or received digital payments in the past year according to the 2017 Global Findex data.[33]

This improvement in financial inclusion does not necessarily translate into access to finance for setting up a business, however. Just 1.5% of the population has borrowed to start, operate, or expand a farm or business and among the bottom 40% of the population, the share drops to 0.5%. (World Bank, 2018) This is less than half the rate of the next lowest peer country and may indicate there are barriers for microenterprises and SMEs to borrow. Access to financial accounts by women is just 60% that of men, which may keep many women from entrepreneurship and SME options, consigning them to low-productivity self-employment.

The IFC (2017) notes that microfinance plays an important role in addressing the needs of the small business sector, especially firms in rural areas that are in dire need of affordable loans, with demand for microfinance services considerably exceeding supply. The IFC provided finance to microfinance institutions in Kazakhstan to expand access to credit to micro and small companies and entrepreneurs, and provided advisory services to improve operational efficiency of microfinance institutions. IFC provided a syndicated loan of $82 million equivalent in Kazakh tenge to "microfinance organization "KMF" LLC to boost lending to micro and small enterprises, including women entrepreneurs and customers in rural areas of Kazakhstan. KMF is the largest private microfinance organization in Kazakhstan. The company operates through 114 offices and has over 250,000 active clients.

According to the register of microfinance institutions (MFIs) of the NBK on 1 January 2018, 149 organizations were operating in the country. The loan portfolio of microfinance organizations as of 1 January 2018, excluding the reserves, amounted to T159,937 million ($485 million). This represents a 58% increase since 2017. According to the Committee of Statistics of the Ministry of National Economy of the Republic of Kazakhstan, in 2017, 614,342 microcredits were issued for a total amount of T228,252 million ($692,000), which is 61% more than in 2016. According to the data of the CS MES RK, 99% of microcredits were issued to individuals, of which 47% of microcredits were officially issued for entrepreneurial purposes. The number of MFIs for 2017 increased by 13 organizations. MFIs are represented in all regions of Kazakhstan, over 60% registered in Almaty City, South Kazakhstan region and Nur-Sultan.

The 2019 Amendments to the Law on Microfinance Activities will help the previously unregulated, microcredit market to work more transparently under the supervision of the National Bank. The increase in the minimum authorized capital up to T100 million will force consolidation in the sector. Important changes include the requirement to provide information on loans issued to borrowers to a credit bureau and the more than doubling of the size of loans that MFIs can issue to their clients to up to T50.5 million (compared to the current T20.2 million). The latter should lead to expand potential borrowers to not only small, but also medium-sized and large businesses.[34]

---

[33] Global Partnership for Financial Inclusion. Kazakhstan. http://datatopics.worldbank.org/g20fidata/country/kazakhstan

[34] Association of Microfinance Associations of Kazakhstan. Kapital.kz: Almost 50% of MFIs do not have the required authorized capital under the new law. http://en.amfok.kz/news/321.html

Foreign Direct Investment

Kazakhstan has performed well in attracting FDI into its economy. FDI has played an important role in Kazakhstan's modern history, accounting for about 50% of the country's GDP throughout the 2000s (OECD, 2017). By 2018, total inward FDI stock in Kazakhstan amounted to $149,253 million, up from only $10,077 million in 2000. According to the Kazakhstan's national statistical office, in 2017, foreign enterprises operating in the country accounted for 61% of industrial output, 66.2% of total exports, and 5.4% of total employment. However, most of the foreign investments—70% of total FDI stock—have been directed into natural resource extraction.

Over the period of 2008–2018 FDI inflows have shown a strong cyclicality, reaching peaks in 2008 (of $14.3 billion) and 2011–12 ($14 billion). Since then, however, FDI inflows in Kazakhstan have fallen sharply, primarily due to the reduced profitability of the domestic oil sector at lower oil prices but also reduced liquidity of firms in other sectors in the aftermath of the crisis (OECD, 2017). In some sectors like banking, there have been departures of several large global players.

The sectoral allocation of inward FDI flows has been geared toward the primary sectors (Figure 26). The principal challenge remains to attract investment into sectors and activities other than natural resource extraction as well as retain investors already present in the economy. In this regard, a joint IFC and World Bank private sector diagnostic study has identified Kazakhstan's wheat, livestock, and transport and logistics sectors to have great potential to increase private sector investment, create new markets, and boost job creation. Kazakhstan is the critical pillar in two of the proposed six economic corridors under the PRC-led Belt and Road Initiative, namely the New Eurasian Land Bridge, connecting the PRC and Europe via Central Asia, and the the PRC-Central Asia-West Asia Corridor. Both initiatives foresee investments up to the $40 billion until 2020 in logistics, public services, SMEs and other infrastructure. The extent to which these result in generating export opportunities could also help stimulate investment in productive capacity.

Beyond the scale of private investment alone, the way it is invested matters for the type of national development path a country follows. The types of industries and jobs created, the skills demanded and nurtured and, particularly around foreign investment, the links with local businesses made can determine the extent to which national productivity and economic growth rises, but also have much wider impacts on incomes, society and the environment.

As well as the scale and type of FDI, the way that countries attract it can also affect its sustainable development impact. One important mechanism through which this occurs is the tax incentives, breaks and holidays offered to investors. These directly reduce the revenues that government receive, thereby limiting the benefit of investment on public finances and reducing the volume of funds available for public services and investment. In general, there is increasing international evidence that much of this tax competition is harmful and unnecessary.

Through corporate social responsibility (CSR) multinational enterprises operating in Kazakhstan could also contribute more directly to specific development outcomes in the close vicinity of their operations. However, while the concept of CSR has undoubtedly gained prominence in Kazakhstan in the last 10 years, Kazakhstan does not have a comprehensive policy to promote CSR (UNECE, 2019). Current efforts are not sufficient if Kazakhstan wishes to have the business community more profoundly engaged in adopting behaviors that lead to sustainable development and support the attainment of the SDGs, regarding its environmental targets.[35]

---

[35] UNDP's "SDG Impact" (https://sdgimpact.undp.org/) was set up for this purpose.

Figure 26. Sectoral Allocation of Foreign Direct Investments over 2013–2018

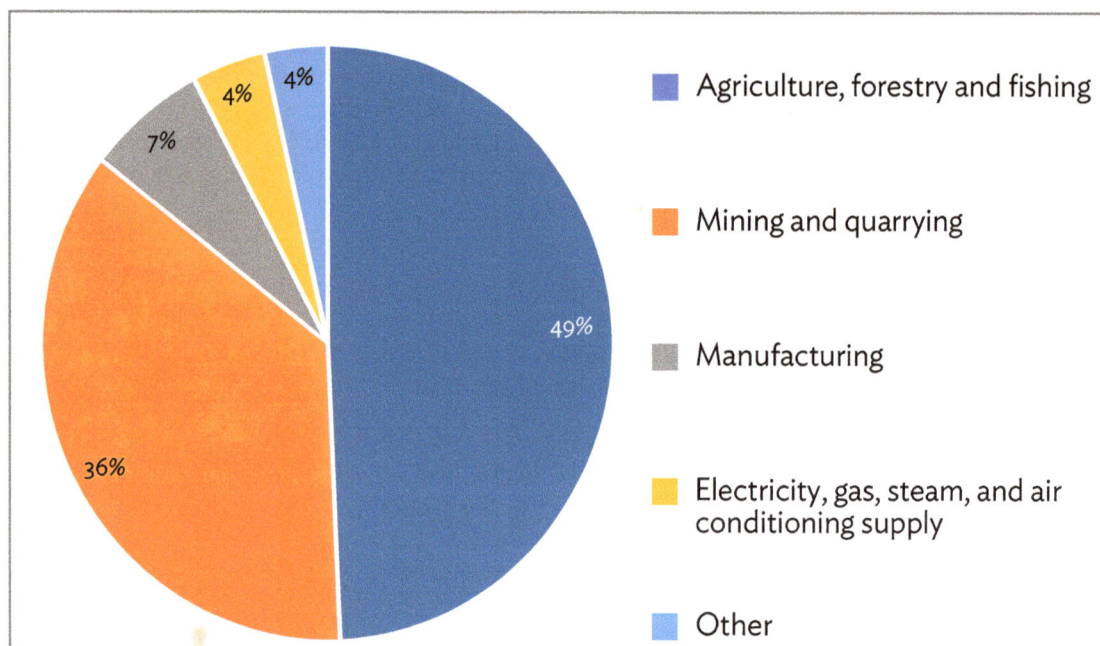

- Agriculture, forestry and fishing
- Mining and quarrying
- Manufacturing
- Electricity, gas, steam, and air conditioning supply
- Other

Source: National Bank of Kazakhstan.

Remittances

Remittances represent a stable, albeit very minor source of development finance in Kazakhstan. However, migrant workers and the remittances they send may be vital to underpin remote, rural communities across the country. There is no further detailed information to analyze the use of remittances and their contribution to national development outcomes. However, since labor migration flows in the region tend to increase, and the volume of inward remittances increase, it becomes much more urgent to use the remittances not only for consumption, but also for development. One approach to increase the developmental impact of remittances is by reducing the cost of sending remittances. Alternatively, diaspora bonds may allow for the country's diaspora to channel their savings into productive investments in their home country.

Philanthropy

Philanthropic organizations play a critical role in providing services to and as advocates for the poorest and most vulnerable communities, people, and environments. There is only anecdotal information readily available on the activities of domestic and international philanthropists or foundations in Kazakhstan. For example, in 2017 Grameen Crédit Agricole Foundation disbursed $5.7 million to the microcredit institution Asian Credit Fund LLC (ACF). ACF's financial services are designed to promote the development of rural households, the growth of small businesses, and home ownership in cities and villages throughout Kazakhstan. With its headquarters in Almaty, ACF has a network of rural offices throughout the country. While these amounts, may appear small relative to the other, major available sources of development finance to Kazakhstan, they may fulfill niche areas of development that are not currently covered by the government.

Dimension 2: Integrated Planning and Financing

The previous chapter shed light on the recent developments of Kazakhstan's development finance landscape. It found that total available development finance declined relative to the country's GDP during the past decade, despite a slight increase of the absolute amounts of development finance. Over the same period there has also been an increasing reliance on domestic public finance. Meeting the country's infrastructure investment needs and sustained social spending will require bucking both trends.

This chapter explores how Kazakhstan's planning and finance policy functions are aligned. It considers both opportunities for strengthening the connection between the annual and/or medium-term budget process with long-term plans as well as alignment across different finance policies such as the budget, private sector development, green development, etc. Stronger integration of Kazakhstan's planning and financing processes can be a first practical step toward developing an integrated national financing framework and strengthening the country's SDG financing mechanisms.

PLANNING FOR DEVELOPMENT OUTCOMES

System of State Planning in Kazakhstan

Kazakhstan has developed a formal system of state planning, documents, processes, concepts, and doctrines that collectively ensure the country's socioeconomic development over the medium- and long-term. The state planning documents are hierarchically grouped according to three levels (Figure 27).

The Strategy Kazakhstan-2050 and the Strategic Development Plan until the year 2025 constitute the top-level planning documents, along with corresponding national key indicators and indicators that define the country's long-term development. The Strategy Kazakhstan-2050, announced by the President in 2012, defines the long-term strategic goals for the country's development. It aims to position Kazakhstan among the world's 30 most developed economies by 2050, by transforming the country into a diversified, knowledge-based economy, with strong domestic production, decent conditions for vulnerable people and modern health care and education. All medium-and short-term national, sectoral and regional development documents are developed in accordance with the Strategy Kazakhstan-2050. The 10-year Strategic Development Plan of the Republic of Kazakhstan 2025 sets out the country's medium-term development priorities. It envisages a combination of seven systemic reforms and seven priority policies for the implementation of Strategy Kazakhstan-2050. Priority reforms cover the development of human capital, technological advance to achieve greater competitiveness, strengthening of the rule of law, regional development and urbanization, the modernization of public consciousness, and greater efficiency in the public sector.

The secondary level of planning documents addresses medium-term development priorities and approaches. These include the "socio-economic development forecast of the Republic of Kazakhstan" for the 5-year period and thematic and sectoral state programs for 5-year periods. A total of 12 cross-cutting

Figure 27. System of State Planning in Kazakhstan

Level 1	1. The Strategy Kazakhstan-2050 2. RK Development Plan until the year of 2025 3. Prospective scheme of territorial and spatial development 4. National Safety Strategy of the RK	4 documents
Level 2	5. Socio-Economic Development Forecast for 2019-2023 6. State Programmes: SPND,Nurly Zhol, Nurly Zher, Business Map 2020, Yenbek, State programme for Agribusinesses Development, Digital Kazakhstan, National Export Strategy of the RK, Regions Development Programme until the year 2020, Densaulyk, UNDP, State Programme for Languages Development	13 documents
Level 3	7. Strategic plans of state bodies 8. Programmes of territorial Development	34 documents
Level 4	• Message by the head of the state to the people of Kazakhstan (Nationwide Plan) • Official instructions by the head of the state • Official instructions by the Prime Minister • Official instructions by the Deputy Prime Minister, ministers, vice-ministers	⊠ documents

Source: TALAP Center for Applied Research, 2019.

state programs complete the secondary level of planning documents. They cover development targets and indicators of sectors and subsectors aimed at achieving the national key targets and indicators.

Third-level documents define how to achieve the first and second level documents of the State Planning System and include 5-year strategic documents of state bodies and ministries (2017–2021), 5-year strategic documents of territorial development programs (2016–2020). In addition, in accordance with Government Decree 790 dd 29.11.17, the development strategies and development plans of SOEs (Sovereign Wealth Fund Samruk-Kazyna, "Baiterek" National Managing Holding and national companies) are also part of the level III documents.

Moreover, the President's Annual Message sets out the policy priorities for the next year, which are reinforced through the government's annual action plan. In addition, the President has announced several cross-cutting development programs, concepts and doctrines[36] to address the country's pressing emerging socio-economic needs. Examples include the adoption of a new concept on the transition to a green economy in 2013. The Nurly Zhol ("bright path") program, announced in 2014, focuses on ambitious infrastructure development; while the "100 Concrete Steps" announced in 2015 specifies a series of measures in various institutional spheres aimed at achieving a "modern state for all. The government has also promoted several flagship policy areas, notably increasing renewable energy supply, improving water efficiency and reducing GHG emissions.

Considering the abundance of planning documents and at times duplication of national and sectoral programs the World Bank (2018) argues that there is a need for stability of priorities and a tighter focus on implementation. More recently, this annual policy guidance from the political elite (represented as the

---

[36] Concepts are of ideological nature to provide a long-term vision of development for a relevant industry along with specifications to guide public policy. A doctrine is a document that defines a set of political principles on specific issues, such as military doctrine or the doctrine on national unity.

"true level" in Figure 26) has tended to skew the policy priorities adopted in the comprehensive set of state planning documents. The President's Annual Message has served to fast-track counter-cyclical spending in the wake of the 2014 oil price decline or to assuage recent social grievances by underpinning social spending. These emerging, short-term policy priorities eventually translate into ad hoc budgetary decisions and revisions which risk undermining the implementation of Kazakhstan's long-term development plans. Articulating a clear long-term vision on resource needs and their strategic allocation could support more stable budgeting practices and long-term fiscal sustainability.

Overall, Kazakhstan performs relatively well in visioning for results, but needs to keep improving its results-based budgeting, implementation and monitoring systems. The OECD (2014) also finds the need for strengthening citizen and business engagement in the long-term visioning and planning process, linking evaluation of policy and program effectiveness more directly back to the results-based budgeting and the resource allocation process.

Strengthening Inclusive Public Finance Processes

Strengthening relations with citizens is a sound investment in better policy making and a core element of good governance. Besides provision of information, the government would need to create an enabling space for consultation and active citizen participation in policy formulation and the decision-making process (OECD, 2001).

Many governments and all major international institutions, such as the IMF[37] and OECD,[38] consider civic engagement in inclusive public finance processes as good practice, and civic organizations in more than 50 countries have established capacity to engage systematically in fiscal policy issues. Evidence[39] from these efforts shows that civic engagement in transparent budget processes has helped to deliver more transparent and equitable, SDG-aligned public finance systems and expenditures across diverse countries and contexts. More specifically, civic participation in budget processes has

- Pushed for greater budget transparency and ensured that citizen priorities receive due consideration during budget decision-making, enhancing equity;

- Promoted budget legitimacy, since citizens feel heard in the budget process when civic actors directly engage executives and legislatures on public finance matters; and

- Tracked budget implementation by ensuring that funds come from and go where they are meant to, thus increasing revenue and spending efficiency and effectiveness.

While there are formal rules[40] and mechanisms in place to facilitate participation of civil society and businesses in decision-making the prevailing impression is that the changes in the decision-making process have thus far been more formal than actual. The planning system and control from the central administration leave limited room for maneuver to the ministries to accommodate multi-stakeholder

---

[37] IMF Fiscal Transparency Code. https://www.imf.org/external/np/fad/trans/Code2019.pdf

[38] OECD. Principles of Budgetary Governance. http://www.oecd.org/gov/budgeting/principles-budgetary-governance.htm

[39] IBP. DFI. Oxfam. 2014. From Numbers to Nurses--Why Budget Transparency, Expenditure Monitoring, and Accountability are Vital to the Post-2015 Framework. Budget Brief. October. https://www.internationalbudget.org/wp-content/uploads/Budget-Brief-From-Numbers-to-Nurses.pdf

[40] Between 2002 and 2011, the government of Kazakhstan directed two programs toward the development of civil society representation: the "Concept of State Support for Non-Commercial Organisations" (2002-2006) and the "Concept of Civil Society Development" (2006-2011).

consultations. In most cases, the objectives of a regulation are indeed determined before any multi-stakeholder consultation has taken place. Acknowledging that external persons and organizations, including those with dissenting views, should play a role in governmental decision-making requires a cultural change in the administration—one that needs to be enforced in practice (OECD, 2014c). In addition, only a fraction of the 30,000 officially registered nongovernment organizations (NGOs) in Kazakhstan is operational and effective (Bertelsmann, 2018).

Aligning Kazakhstan's Development Plan with the Sustainable Development Goals

The 2030 Agenda coincides to a large extent with the country's development priorities as identified in the Strategy Kazakhstan-2050, the 2025 Strategic Development Plan, the Plan of the Nation, "100 concrete steps to Implement Five Institutional Reforms," the Five Social Initiatives of the Head of State and the "Ruhani Jangyru" program. These programs and initiatives are aimed at strengthening human capital, creating a sustainable economy, and improving the quality of life across all segments of the population.

The State Planning System serves the purpose of implementing the SDGs at national level. Today, about 79.9% of the SDG targets are already reflected in the documents of the national planning system of Kazakhstan (RIA, 2019).

There is a strong commitment from the highest political level to the 2030 Agenda. The Government of Kazakhstan created a "Coordination Council on Sustainable Development Goals" to oversee the implementation of the SDGs in Kazakhstan. It is chaired by the deputy prime minister, with five intersectoral working groups, dedicated for the "5 Ps" of SDGs – People, Prosperity, Planet, Peace, and Partnership, each enjoying participation of civil society, private sector and other stakeholders to integrate the views of all stakeholders in emerging policies and decisions. MNE is the coordinating body of the Council, supported by ERI, which provides expert and analytical support, serving as the Secretariat. In July 2019, Kazakhstan presented its first Voluntary National Review (VNR) during the High-Level Political Forum on Sustainable Development.

Following these early successes and progress, it is important to maintain the current SDG momentum by the government to increase the pace of attaining the SDGs. The VNR has set out a series of next steps to improve the national mechanisms to implement the SDGs. These include

- defining both the baseline and target values for SDG indicators up to 2030,

- implementing a monitoring and reporting system for SDG indicators,

- completing the process of nationalizing SDG objectives and indicators,

- harmonizing budget planning with the SDG objectives and indicators.

The ongoing process of nationalizing and localizing the SDG indicators should lead to the mainstreaming of SDG targets and indicators into the state planning system and monitoring mechanism. This process constitutes a critical step to facilitate the alignment of the planning processes with the budgetary processes in Kazakhstan.

ALIGNMENT OF STATE PLANNING SYSTEM WITH BUDGETARY PROCESSES

At the foundation of an INFF is the need for the planning and finance policy functions of government to be closely aligned (Figure 28). This is key to setting out development aspirations that are in step with the policies designed to realize them, and to effectively addressing the challenges and opportunities that finance trends present (UNDP, 2019). The strategic plan and budget should reflect the negotiation between those responsible for budget allocations and those setting the strategic direction of ministries (OECD, 2012). In practice, performance budgeting enables linking between strategic planning and budgeting by translating the development vision into program spending.

In Kazakhstan, the system of public financial management has been the subject of wide- ranging reforms over recent years, aimed at strengthening the capacity to support the country's strategic development.

The overarching goal of budgetary governance in Kazakhstan is to forge clear links between strategic plans of state bodies and budgetary processes. To practically improve the alignment of strategic plans both with the overarching Development Plan and with the budget Kazakhstan has rolled out results-based budgeting in 2016. According to the legal framework and current practice, each ministry and agency should update its 5-year strategic plan at 3-year intervals. Budget programs, together with key performance indicators and targets, covering both current and capital expenditure for the 3 years ahead should be elaborated based on strategic plans. This set-up should ensure aligning the costs of the strategic plans of state bodies with their respective budget programs.

Figure 28. Common Elements of National Planning and Financing Systems

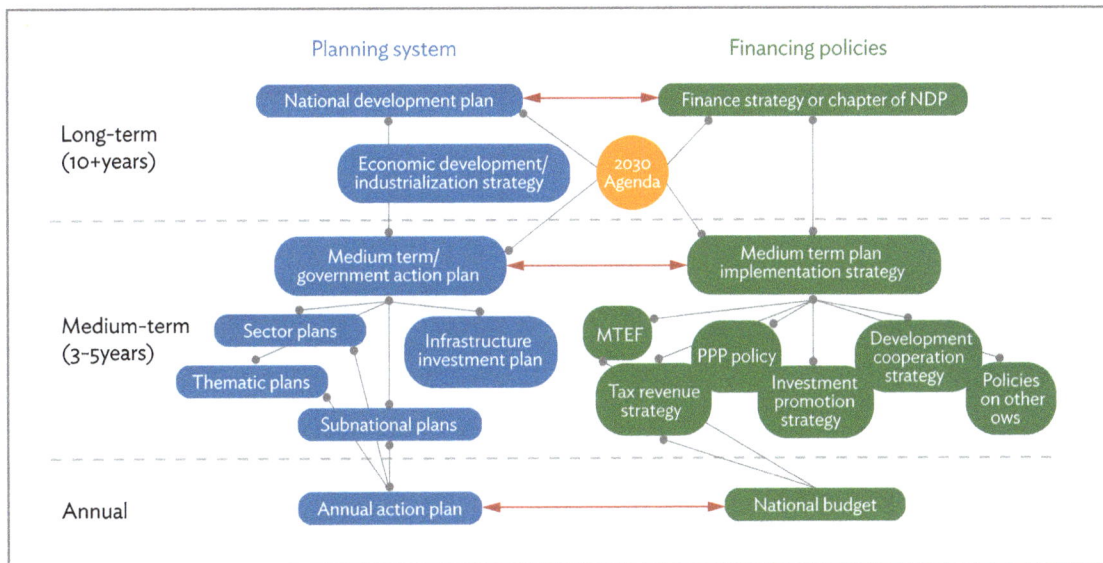

Note: The red arrows highlight key points at which the planning and financing systems should be closely connected. Source: UNDP (2018). Country innovations for integrated SDG financing.

MTEF = Medium-term expenditure framework, NDP = National Development Plan, PPP = private-public partnership
Note: The red arrows highlight key points at which the planning and financing systems should be closely connected.
Source: UNDP. 2018. Country innovations for integrated SDG financing.

While the MNE provides some central guidance and oversight of the development of strategic plans and budget programs, in practice responsibility for the definition of programs, performance indicators and targets is largely devolved to line ministries and agencies. As a result, there is wide variation across ministries both in the number of programs and in the quality of performance indictors and targets. For example, the MNE is responsible for more than 15 programs while some smaller agencies have only one program with no subprograms (OECD, 2019).

The Forecast of Social and Economic Development (FSED) provides a high-level, formal connection between the annual state budget allocations and the country's long-term development prerogatives. The FSED is a rolling 5-year forecast that takes its direction from the Development Strategy Kazakhstan-2050, and the Strategic Development Plan until 2025 and the President's annual message. It is included in the budget package presented to Parliament, along with the main fiscal parameters of the budget; strategic plans of the ministries and the main budget document (OECD, 2019).

Comprehensive reviews by the OECD (2019) and the World Bank (2017) of the country's recent public financial management (PFM) reforms find that strategic planning is well-established throughout government, contributing to a more strategic allocation of resources. The programs set out in each strategic plan are generally aligned with the budget programs of each ministry and managerial responsibility has been clarified in each area. However, they find the quality of the strategic plans and the design of budget programs to be uneven and the strategic plans do not manage to fully reconcile strategic objectives with hard budget constraints.

Both institutions concur in that the de facto implementation of Kazakhstan's State Planning System is not as advanced as it de jure institutional and regulatory framework indicates. They point to the deficient performance monitoring and reporting and the underlying insufficient quality of indicators and targets which varies considerably across ministries and agencies. Ministries with fewer programs generally seem to have better quality key performance indicators, while several policy ministries (e.g, innovation, energy, education, and science) have found it challenging to come up with good quality, relevant indicators (OECD, 2019). It will require a major long-term effort to establish an adequate framework linking strategic planning to performance reporting (World Bank, 2017). The SDG targets and their nationalized and localized indicators could provide a useful framework to inform or use as the setting of appropriate KPIs.

Considering this important finding, the DFA argues that there is an opportunity to connect the ongoing process of nationalizing and localizing the SDG indicators with the authorities' endeavors to improve the monitoring of progress against the national development targets and how state spending contributes to these development outcomes.

The SDG's comprehensive agenda means it provides a relevant, internationally agreed, set of indicators to cover reporting on the three sustainable development dimensions—economic, social, and environmental—across Kazakhstan's development programs and strategies. Thus, the nationalized SDG indicators—soon to be finalized and agreed upon by consensus—can be the key to practically connect strategic development outcomes with public spending through the state budget (Figure 29). This approach would strengthen the SDG implementation mechanism and address the VNR recommendation to create a harmonized monitoring and reporting system for SDG indicators and budget planning.

The MoF's endeavor to digitalize the budget process provides a timely ongoing reform process to which to anchor the improvement of the results-based budget's performance monitoring. Mexico's budgeting for the SDGs provides a highly relevant example for Kazakhstan to learn from and emulate (Box 7).

Figure 29. Harmonized Reporting System for the Sustainable Development Goals and Budget Planning

Several countries have developed PFM strategies designed to strengthen the way public finances are collected and spent, and to deepen alignment with the national development plan and Sustainable Development Goals (SDGs) (Box 4). Governments have developed long-term approaches involving a sequence of iterative reforms that cumulatively build systems that are more efficient and more closely aligned to national objectives. The examples can prompt Kazakhstan considering similar reforms to think about the sequence, time and capacity-building that reforms will require.

Box 4. Country Approaches to Strengthen Linkages Between Strategic Planning and Budgeting

Iterative reforms to public financial management systems in the Philippines and Mozambique give the governments more control over how public resources are invested overall and greater insight into the performance of these investments. Uganda has implemented reforms designed to delegate clear authority to the planning authority to take responsibility for budgetary planning alignment while

Malaysia, the government uses a review mechanism to ensure that budget spending is aligned to the Eleventh Malaysia Plan and, as of 2017, to the SDGs. During the budget preparation process, ministries submit their proposed costed projects to the Economic Planning Unit of the Prime Minister's Department and the Ministry of Finance for review. These projects are then judged against the six strategic thrusts and the national key results areas of the Eleventh Malaysia Plan. For the 2017 budget, which was presented in October 2016, the Economic Planning Unit adapted this process so that submissions from ministries must detail the extent to which their proposed projects contribute toward the targets of the SDGs. Project proposals that further progress toward the SDGs are given higher priority in central government's budget allocations.

Source: UNDP (2019b).

Coherence Across Strategic Planning and the Medium-Term Expenditure Framework

In Kazakhstan, the budget is the largest source of funding for investment designed to explicitly advance national sustainable development objectives. Therefore, its effective allocation and spending is critical for realizing Strategy Kazakhstan-2050 and underlying programs and strategies. The Medium-Term Expenditure Framework (MTEF) is the mechanism that enables to connect the revenue and expenditure projections with the sectoral, ministerial and regional programs and strategies.

Despite the existing setup of a clear and well-observed annual calendar, and framed within a 3-year rolling cycle, the MTEF is not underpinning discussions around strategic resource allocations (OECD, 2019). The outer 2 years of the rolling budget cycle represent indicative rather than binding commitments, which challenges effective planning of multi-year development projects. The MTEF has the potential to be developed into a more significant tool for strategic resource allocation, complementing the Forecast of Social and Economic Development (FSED) by providing a more detailed rationale shifting resources between sectors and within sectors based on alignment with policy priorities.

For the MTEF to underpin strategic resource allocation would require fewer ad hoc, discretionary revisions of budgets and plans. In recent years, the FSED, strategic plans and the budget itself have been subject to multiple revisions during the year as economic and fiscal conditions have been subject to rapid changes. For example, the FSED for 2016–2020 was revised 3 times due to changing global economic conditions. On foot of reforms initiated by the Parliament, from 2018 the major budget revisions are now limited to once per year. It would be advisable for revisions to the strategic plans to move toward a similar degree of stability. The OECD (2019) recommends the 3-year rolling forecasts should develop a more stable and normative character to guide the evolution of the public finances and to support planning within ministries. This requires the annual budget cycle to better align and sequence with the national planning cycle.

Financing Strategy to Ensure Coherence Across Financing Policies

An overarching financing strategy can provide a foundation on which to implement policies related to each type of finance individually and linking them to development outcomes. Such a financing strategy guides the resources and financing instruments that are needed to achieve the long-term national development plan. It provides a basis for managing policy trade-offs between different financial sources and instruments and identifies the changes of a more structural nature that need to be implemented to unlock new sources of finance. The scope of an overarching financing strategy goes beyond the public sources of development finance.

Kazakhstan's state planning system currently does not explicitly identify and direct the scale and types of public and private financing that will be needed to deliver the investments and services required by the national development plan. There would be value in adopting a more strategic approach regarding Kazakhstan's long-term resource needs and the required financing policies to meet these needs. A financing strategy could serve to inform the policy trade-offs, identified in this DFA and also enable identifying synergies between public and private finance flows.

Having a financing strategy entails understanding the challenges and risks to the long-term sustainability of financial resources. Recent macroeconomic shocks have put serious strains on Kazakhstan's budget and depleted the reserves of the National Fund. Prudent management of public finances and strong balance sheets have been critical in enabling the government to use fiscal policy to stabilize economic activity in the short run, for example through increased expenditure on social welfare programs, and promoting economic growth over the longer term. In the longer term, Kazakhstan faces fiscal sustainability challenges arising from its dependence on natural resource revenues and demographic changes. The elderly population will increase from approximately 11% of the population to 15% by 2050, driving up health expenditure requirements (OECD, 2019).

The 10-year Strategic Development Plan of the Republic of Kazakhstan 2025 does not establish indicative long-term finance targets for the different resource flows. These would be quantitative targets for mobilizing the resources needed to provide financial feasibility to the national development strategy. Its MTEF cover only the 3 years immediately ahead, and there are no projections beyond that horizon that would demonstrate how fiscal sustainability is to be maintained, given the development of Kazakhstan's assets and liabilities.

Most of the country's medium-term strategic plans and programs include headline cost estimates of total amount of financial resources required, along with the share of these resources to be provided by the budget and by other commercial, financial resources. It does not specify however, how these headline resource requirements translate into the annual budget process, financing policies, or how the different financing flows contribute to development outcomes. Estimating the implied costs of the national plan allows estimating the financing gap to be addressed and monitor over time how this gap compares with development finance trends.

Recomendations

This third and final chapter summarizes the two key areas of recommendations building on the findings across the previous two analytical chapters. These recommendations are specific to the focus areas of a DFA in that they relate directly to developing the two first INFF building blocks and strengthen the country's SDG financing mechanisms. Using an INFF lens to structure the key recommendations to be taken forward unavoidably leads to leaving out some other relevant recommendations, more tailored to specific financing issues or flows. The underlying rationale being that the retained DFA recommendations should complement, rather than duplicate the more specific, technical areas of recommendation identified in recent analytical works by specialized agencies, e.g. specific tax administration reforms by the IMF or PFM reforms by the World Bank, etc.

It will be important to also identify the institutional arrangements that will be set to take these DFA recommendations forward. Therefore, the recommendations will be presented and discussed among government stakeholders and development partners to align them with current policy priorities and embed them into ongoing reform processes. Such discussion may lead to establishing a road map outlining a clear set of "agreed" and actionable measures for operationalizing the recommendations. This roadmap should also lay out the mechanism for overseeing its implementation.

The overarching, headline recommendation that emerges from this 'light' DFA analysis would be for Kazakhstan to consider the value of adopting an INFF to support its sustainable development strategy. Several findings across both dimensions analyzed point to the potential usefulness of adopting an INFF to inform strategic resource allocations toward achieving development results. The two key areas of recommendations that constitute the remainder of this chapter focus on strengthening the institutional structures required for progressing toward an INFF.

HEADLINE FINDINGS	RECOMMENDATIONS
1. Stagnation of total available development finance 2. Increasing reliance on domestic sources of finance, including domestic commercial investments with a significant share of state-related private sector investment 3. Tensions between long-term fiscal sustainability and social spending 4. Trade-offs between development priorities and financing policies and instruments 5. Disconnect between the long-term development vision and short-term financing policies	Lay out a holistic financing strategy to raise resources, manage risks, and achieve sustainable development priorities: • Estimate resource needs of the development strategy Kazakhstan-2050 and for the 2030 Agenda • Establish financing targets for both public and private resources to meet identified resource needs • Integrate a "DFA Dashboard" in the Forecast of Social and Economic Development • Access untapped sources of climate-related development finance • Reform fossil fuel subsidies • Streamline tax incentives and exemptions according to cost-benefit analyses

Moreover, this DFA could serve the practical purpose of informing a proposal to the SDG Fund for further developing the four building blocks for the design and operationalization of financing frameworks in Kazakhstan. The SDG Fund provides an opportunity for supporting the operationalization of INFFs in several countries and accepts proposals until February 2020 on a "first-come, first-served" basis basis. In line with both DFA dimensions the focus of the proposal would be on developing the INFF building blocks: (i) assessment and diagnostics and (ii) financing strategy.

DEVELOP A HOLISTIC FINANCING STRATEGY

Kazakhstan could consider developing an overarching financing strategy to underpin its SDG financing mechanisms. Such a country-owned financing framework brings together financing and related policies most relevant to addressing a country's financing challenges. It would look at the full range of financing sources and non-financial means of implementation that are available, and lay out a financing strategy to raise resources, manage risks, and achieve sustainable development priorities (UN, 2019). It can provide guidance on how to address the synergies, trade-offs and competing priorities that exist between different aspects of financing sustainable development.

This may require holding discussions at the highest level of government authority first to agree about the benefits of such a financing strategy as well as assessing and presenting the options on how to structure it to meet the objectives of the strategic plans. Thus, providing an initial analysis about the types of finances that can be mobilized and included in it, options on monitoring its implementation and the participation of non-state actors in the whole process.

A practical step toward developing an overarching financing strategy that governs and monitors the different types of development finance would be establishing a single point of focus that governs the overall approach to public and private finance. Such a coordinating focal point would ideally be hosted at MNE considering its role in establishing the FSED. Furthermore, the FSED could be expanded with a development finance dashboard that monitors development finance trends in contrast with Kazakhstan's resource needs (see below). Such a development finance dashboard could monitor progress toward mobilizing the identified resources and how these contribute to development targets and indicators and be integrated in the whole financing strategy implementation monitoring process.

This would also require estimating the resource needs of achieving its long-term development priorities and setting financing targets for both public and private resources. This may involve building government capacity to gauge costs across the SDGs over time, dynamically as progress is made and circumstances change.

Estimate the Cost of Achieving the Long-Term Development Priorities

Establishing broad estimates of the resources—the investments and ongoing spending—needed to realize the vision of a national development plan is an important basis for a structured approach to mobilizing the necessary scale and mix of resources. It is a key building block of an INFF.

For authorities to enable developing a holistic financing strategy requires developing quantitative targets of the resources to be mobilized toward the financial feasibility of the strategy Kazakhstan-2050. Such costing estimates should encompass both the public and private investment needs to be mobilized over time toward Kazakhstan's national development outcomes. Such estimates should account for the synergies and trade-offs between investments in interconnected areas of sustainable development.

Practically, this may require starting by undertaking mid- and long-term costing exercises to initially inform the suggested process or establishing cost estimates of specific sectoral or thematic priority interventions. This approach might be relevant to discuss and consider the benefits of costing long-term development priorities and making these a standardized part of the policy development process. Eventually, if taken forward, the aim would be to periodically cost the 10-year strategic plan, which informs and guides all underlying medium-term strategic programs and plans.

Other DFAs found that country estimates of resource needs are typically based on projections of current financing trends into the future. However, a complementary approach to understanding the resource needs would be to 'backcast' from a desired status of the economy—the one that would provide general feasibility to the national plans—to the present state and defining the main stages in this process, key milestones, and specific targets for individual finance flows (APDEF, 2017).

Cambodia, Malaysia, and Thailand have all developed estimates of the scale of financing needed to realize their medium-term (4–5 year) plans. These include varying degrees of detail on which to delineate responsibilities and objectives into targets and policies for different types of finance. Bangladesh and Nepal have undertaken exercises to estimate the cost of achieving the SDGs, looking at both public and private resources. These countries could provide opportunities for south-south cooperation and peer learning on how to develop costing models for their national development plans.

Establish Financing Targets for Both Public and Private Resources

Establishing long-term finance goals enables monitoring how the current financing trends compare to the required resource needs as estimated in Strategic Development Plan and take corrective policy actions if required.

It would also allow a qualitative assessment of how different finance flows contribute to national development targets, on the condition that finance flows are incorporated into the hierarchical monitoring frameworks that link government policy and program outputs to outcomes, and outcomes to headline national development targets.

Financing targets can be both quantitative and qualitative. The most obvious quantitative financing targets revenue targets would be targets for revenue or tax collection, often relative to GDP. But it could also involve setting targets for mobilizing private resources and actors to finance specific development priorities in infrastructure, health or education. Qualitative financing targets would, for example, increase the redistributive impact of Kazakhstan's fiscal system or ensuring that the private resources align more to national priorities such as reducing inequality. The Solomon Islands Integrated Financing Framework provide another relevant example: they have outlined specific policy actions in the short and medium-term based on the articulation of strategic (qualitative) directions for each type of development finance flow or relevant financing instrument.

Integrate a "DFA Dashboard" into the Annual Forecast of Social and Economic Development

Integrating a DFA module with the outlook of all development finance flows into the 5-year, rolling forecast for socioeconomic developments to monitor progress against meeting the long-term resource needs. A DFA dashboard would provide a practical link between the development strategy's long-term resource needs with the medium-term financing trends and financing approach. It would allow the government to maintain a current understanding of the financing landscape, to strengthen the understanding of the impacts that different resources make toward national priorities and to adjust prioritization and adapt policy design in a more responsive and timely way.

The DFA dashboard would have to be included both in the State Planning System and in the budgeting process. It would thus be part of the "budget package" to be provided to Parliament in the form of a 2-page strategic assessment of the development finance landscape to inform decision-making.

The DFA dashboard could also be used to build up statistical capacity and strengthen institutional linkages across relevant state bodies. The broad range of data that underpins the DFA analysis would have to be centralized, updated and provided by the Statistics Committee, relying on medium-term revenue and expenditure data from the MoF, NBK, and other relevant domestic sources. The DFA analysis could be undertaken by the ERI, as the Secretariat of the SDG Coordination council, thus providing for a connection between Kazakhstan's SDG implementation mechanism and the state planning and budgeting system.

Access Untapped Sources of Climate-Related Development Finance

There are indications that Kazakhstan is not maximizing the potential of climate-related development finance to finance its economic transition away from natural resource-dependence economic transformation. Climate related development finance does not only provide additional funding, but typically comes with technical assistance and sector-specific know-how and networks. Climate-related development finance has evolved into a highly complex ecosystem, which can be challenging to navigate for interested countries. Kazakhstan could rely on its development partners present in the country to support them developing an effective strategy to maximize the development potential of climate funding. Priority actions to consider are:

• The Ministry of Environment in conjunction with the MoF could perform a systematic qualitative and quantitative analysis of Kazakhstan's public expenditures and how they relate to climate change, in the form of a Climate Public Expenditure and Institutional Review. This could inform a more holistic and effective government approach toward mitigating and adapting to climate change.

• There's an opportunity to tap into the Green Climate Fund (GCF)—the world largest climate fund, largely underrepresented in Central Asia—which focuses on greenhouse gas emissions reductions and adapting to climate change. This would require using GCF's funding as a tool to leverage additional private investment toward transformative climate mitigation actions. Adopting a regional approach, while more complex, would greatly enhance the chances of success. ADB, the EBRD, and the World Bank all are accredited entities of the GCF and would be relevant partners to support developing a road map for Kazakhstan to access GCF funding.

• The recently launched 2050 Almaty city development strategy provides an opportunity to implement environmental sustainability programmes stipulated within that strategy, considering this region's catastrophic air pollution situation. This could serve as a pilot for standardizing an effective approach of cooperation with development partners in climate finance across the country.

Reform Fossil Fuel Subsidies to Finance Social Expenditure

The structurally low oil prices and the real depreciation of the tenge provide a window of opportunity to reduce inefficient fossil fuel subsidies. Kazakhstan may take advantage of these relatively low oil prices to take stronger steps to reform energy subsidies and free up fiscal space for better-targeted social spending or shift additional resources to tradable sectors (World Bank, 2018). Box 5 provides key elements of successful comprehensive subsidy reforms conducted in other countries.

The benefits of addressing fossil fuel subsidies may support achieving greater fiscal and environmental sustainability. Reforming fossil fuel subsidies is part of global action aimed at cutting government spending on fuels that contribute to greenhouse gas emissions and pollutants. Fuel subsidies, if targeted well, can help ease the burden of international oil prices on the poor; on the other hand, these budgets tend to increase over time undermining government's efforts to ensure fiscal sustainability. Phasing out subsidies enables to gradually increase fiscal space and to redirect funding to essential public investments in education, health or infrastructure. Finally, fossil fuel subsidies create disincentives for the development of renewable energy, by making the latter less competitive. These potential benefits need to be weighed against the possible short-term impact on Kazakhstan's overall energy balance and key cities and regions in Northern Kazakhstan for which coal remains important. In the longer run, fossil fuel reduction may have to go hand in hand with sectoral or industrial redevelopment in these areas.

More broadly, beyond energy subsidies, an important step toward understanding the benefits of subsidy reforms in Kazakhstan may be to shed light on the total amounts and mechanisms utilized to channel different subsidies to specific groups of the population or economic sectors. For instance, subsidies may be channeled directly through the state budget, local governments, state-owned enterprises, joint-stock companies or indirectly through subsidized lending by the banking sector. Targeted sectors range from the agriculture sector to SME financing. This creates a complex system that renders it very difficult to assess the true impact of the subsidies on state budgets, on inequality, poverty reduction as well as their economic efficiency. Furthermore, this lack of transparency because subsidies are not overseen solely by the state budget, undermines effective and transparent communication required to underpin any subsidy reform strategy.

Box 5. Key Elements of a Comprehensive Energy Subsidy Reform

Formulate an integrated reform strategy by better aligning energy prices to market and cost recovery levels to reduce budgetary costs in gradual manner

- Create incentives to reduce energy intensity and inefficiency

- Reduce existing leaks to privileged segments of the population while strengthening the focus on vulnerable segments through better registry systems and better targeted social safety nets.

- Ensure predictability by refraining from ad hoc adjustments.

Source: IMF; 2018b.

Streamline Tax Incentives and Exemptions

A thorough examination of the tax incentive system in Kazakhstan is needed. Considering Kazakhstan's low tax ratio and limited fiscal space there is a clear tradeoff between giving tax incentives that result in revenue loss and improving the infrastructure by using those foregone tax revenues. The World Bank (2017) recommends the tax incentives' system in Kazakhstan to be rationalized, linked to the size of investment and better targeted to reducing investment costs, such as accelerated depreciation, investment tax credit, rather than opaque and outright tax exemptions.

A first step would be to introduce tax expenditure reporting (a growing number of countries report estimates in their annual budgets now) and periodic cost-benefit analyses that look at how effective incentives are in mobilizing investments that contribute toward national sustainable development objectives. The latter could eventually evolve into a more formal mechanism for monitoring and managing tax incentives toward ensuring they represent value for money.

STRENGTHEN THE SDG FINANCING MECHANISMS

HEADLINE FINDINGS	RECOMMENDATIONS
6. Weak links between planning and budgeting processes 7. Unclear how public spending contributes to progress against the Sustainable Development Goals (SDGs) 8. Uneven implementation of results-based budgeting across ministries 9. Low quality of the key performance indicators for the budget programs planning documents 10. Strategic planning remains largely top-down, with limited, effective contributions by civil society and business	Strengthen linkages between the state planning system, the budgeting process and the SDGs: • Integrate the nationalized SDG indicators across state planning system and the budget process • Introduce SDG budgeting • Broadening participation of non-state actors in the budget or policy development process

Embed Nationalized Sustainable Development Goal Indicators into Kazakhstan's Respective Development Strategies and Plans to Allow for Monitoring Progress Toward Development Outcomes

Kazakhstan is currently finalizing the nationalization and localization of the SDG indicators. This final set of agreed, comprehensive indicators provides an opportunity to strengthen the performance monitoring of State Planning System across its underlying national strategies and development programs.

At the same time, there is an opportunity to integrate the nationalized SDG indicators into the results-based budgeting process to underpin its performance monitoring: the ongoing digitalization of the budget provides a timely opportunity to consider linking the SDGs to the state budget. Mexico provides a relevant example of how to strengthen budgeting for the SDGs.

Having the SDG indicators linked with both the strategic planning and the state budget process would provide a mechanism to strengthen the governance mechanisms that align policies and annual budgets to the national development plan. Subsequently, this architecture could inform how the state budget is contributing to the SDGs. The SDG coordination council should host an annual multi-stakeholder event to discuss the funding of the SDGs by the state budget and how it underpins progress to the country's development outcomes.

Introduce SDG Budgeting

As the primary political and economic expression of government policy, the budget is a natural starting point for the integration of 2030 Agenda and its SDGs. The benefit of SDG bugeting is that it could serve to improve Kazakhstan's budget performance evaluation system or as a management tool for resource allocation and arbitration. Using the SDGs as a negotiation tool in the budgetary process should keep in mind two facts: (i) many targets cannot be achieved simply by the addition of more money. They also require policies, public norms and regulations; (ii) SDGs should be used not only to address the question: "how much should we spend and where?"; but also "how can we spend it better?"

Analyzing other countries' experience shows that the SDGs and the objectives they support must be recognized as a national priority on the political agenda. Indicators can be used as tools for steering public action if they are used at all stages of public policy making, both upstream to legitimize and institutionalize a phenomenon and to monitor its evolution, and downstream to evaluate the results of a policy strategy. This requires parliamentarians, civil society, other political parties and ministries to use the SDGs to improve the budget debate (Box 6). Only then can budgeting processes play a role in putting the SDGs into politics by providing a forum for debate between the different actors and interest groups (Hege and Brimont 2018).

Box 6. Important Characteristics to Ensure That SDG Integration Into Budgetary Processes is a Useful Exercise

The first relates to the broader Sustainable Development Goals (SDGs) implementation strategy of a country. To what extent does a government translate the broad SDG framework to suit its national context and sustainable development challenge? The SDGs require some translation to adapt to the national context before becoming sufficiently operational for their integration into a State budget. It is easier to link the SDGs to the budget if there is a national implementation plan or strategy that formulates national priorities. These priorities can be cross-sectoral. High-level political support is an important condition for success.

1. The degree of involvement of finance ministries. Is such a ministry piloting or supporting the exercise? A Ministry of Finance could use the SDGs as a management tool to negotiate on allocations and to avoid conflicts within the overall State budget. Do ministries voice their concerns on some SDGs and use them to defend their proposals and fight for their budget share?

2. To impact the political debate and increase accountability, it is essential that the tools developed are taken up by actors such as non-governmental organizations, parliamentarians and supreme audit institutions, as these actors are crucial in holding governments to account regarding their commitments to the Agenda 2030.

Source: Hege and Brimont 2018.

Box 7. SDG Budgeting in Mexico

The Office of the President, the National Institute of Statistics and Geography and the Ministry of Finance, with the support from the United Nations Development Programme, have sought to define and develop mechanisms to link Mexico's budget with the Sustainable Development Goals (SDGs). The purpose was to identify specific budget items and estimate the allocation sufficient to contribute to progress on the SDGs, using a results-based management perspective.

Given the current indirect link between budgets and SDGs, Mexico used key elements of its institutional architecture to strengthen the connection:

1. National planning;
2. Programmatic structure based on budgetary programmes;
3. The performance evaluation system; and
4. Accounting harmonisation.

Building on this, two main steps have been taken:

1) Linking: each ministry has applied the performance evaluation system and national planning to match their programmes to the SDGs;

2) Quantifying: programmes that contribute to each SDG target were identified indicating a direct or indirect contribution to estimate the total investment per target and overall. 102 SDG targets were further disaggregated by different topics (sub-goals), allowing a more precise indication of any sub-goal to which a programme is linked.

Because of this process, Mexico has improved information to:

- Identify the link between the current national planning (medium-term) and the long-term SDGs;
- Assess the percentage of SDGs linked to government programmes and, conversely, the number of programmes linked to each SDG;
- Communicate the country's starting point and what has been achieved;
- Make public policy decisions and budget allocations based on an initial analysis of how much is currently invested in each SDG.

Source: OECD (2018), «Country profiles: Institutional mechanisms for policy coherence», in Policy Coherence for Sustainable Development 2018: Towards Sustainable and Resilient Societies, OECD Publishing, Paris, https://doi.org/10.1787/9789264301061-6-en.

A first step toward introducing SDG budgeting would be to map the budget against the SDGs along with qualitative reporting on how the budget is linked to different SDGs. This is the scope of the RIA exercise of the national budget, being undertaken in parallel to this DFA. This mapping could be performed annually on the proposed budget submitted to Parliament to inform policy discussion on the SDGs. Kazakhstan can consider the Mexico's SDG budgeting approach (Box 7) and assess its feasibility for adopting it in Kazakhstan.

SDG budgeting provides a mechanism to strengthen the linkages between planning and budgeting in

Kazakhstan and formally include the MoF to Kazakhstan's SDG's implementation mechanism. The latter has so far been organized from within the MNE, with oversight by the Prime Minister's Office and the Presidential Cabinet. The key to connect planning with budgeting is through using the SDGs international performance indicators in combination with the nationalized SDG indicators to monitor both progress against planning as well as budgetary performance. The advantage of replacing national performance indicators with international ones is to allow international comparability—provided that other countries do the same—which thus increases accountability. Secondly, the 2030 Agenda provides a long-term framework, and its indicators give some stability and credibility to the evaluation system compared to national indicators that can be changed according to politicians' changing priorities.

Within the MoF this process may have to be instigated by the office in charge of budget performance monitoring, in close coordination with the MNE department responsible for performance monitoring within the state planning system. The ongoing digitalization of the budgetary processes provides a timely opportunity for the MoF to consider integrating the SDG indicators within its budgetary performance processes and lay the foundation for a formal link with the planning system.

Broaden the Participation of Non-State Actors

Integrating the SDGs into budgeting processes faces similar challenges to attempts to incorporate new wealth indicators into the budgetary discussion: indicators can be used as tools for steering public action if they are used at all stages of public policymaking, both upstream to legitimize and institutionalize a phenomenon and to monitor its evolution, and downstream to evaluate the results of a policy strategy (Hege, 2018). Therefore, the SDGs and the objectives they support must be recognized as a national priority on the political agenda. This requires parliamentarians, civil society, other political parties and ministries to use the SDGs to improve the budget debate. Only then can budgeting processes play a role in putting the SDGs into politics by providing a forum for debate between the different actors and interest groups.

There is a strong appetite by Kazakh civil society to inform policymaking in Kazakhstan and support the 2030 Agenda. During a consultation with civil society by the World Bank for their Systematic Country Diagnostic participants expressed appreciation for the opportunity to comment on the objectives and priorities of the draft partnership framework as well as the World Bank's ongoing commitment to ensuring that its work was appropriately informed by citizen engagement and the views of critical stakeholders. They also suggested a role for development partners in building the capacity of civil society to monitor and contribute to the shaping of government policy and performance.

For civil society to execute their SDG accountability function requires forging links between budgets and SDGs. The soon-to-be finalized nationalized SDG indicator framework can reveal the progress of Kazakhstan toward the SDGs and help assess the government's performance. This involves adopting the nationalized SDG indicator across all existing and new government development plans and strategic programs as well as in its performance-based budgeting processes. Thus, the SDGs would serve as an evaluation framework to provide a more comprehensive assessment of budget proposals and therefore increase transparency for nongovernment actors, notably Parliament and civil society, but also the business community. It is important to note that this greatly depends on what is presented and measured: budget allocations, actual spending, results, etc.

Moreover, the civil society can support authorities with translating the SDGs into a more recognizable, down-to-earth set of issues that citizens' daily lives and their societal problems. The SDGs are formulated as problems to resolve by 2030, organizing and reporting on the budget around these goals might be more attractive for citizens than organizing it around thematic areas like education, etc. In line with the 2019 VNR SDGs are consistent with Kazakhstan's development efforts and can serve as a useful and convincing strategic basis for solving national problems.

One practical approach to be considered is thinking of the SDGs as a basis for developing a budget-reporting dashboard for citizens. Such an approach, and the underlying comprehensive assessment of how budget proposals and development plans align with the SDG targets would ideally be impulse and monitored by the Coordination Board of the SDGs and executed by the different multi-stakeholder SDG Working Groups.

References

Alvaredo, F. et al. 2018. World Inequality Report 2018. World Inequality Lab.

Asia Pacific Development Effectiveness Facility. 2017. Financing the Sustainable Development Goals in ASEAN. https://asean.org/wp-content/uploads/2012/05/Report-on-Financing-SDGs-in-ASEAN1.pdf

Asian Development Bank. 2019. Key Indicators for Asia and the Pacific. Manila.

Babajanian, B., Hagen-Zanker, J., and Salomon H. 2015. Analysis of Social Transfers for Children and their Families in Kazakhstan. UNICEF.

Bertelsmann Stiftung. 2014. Bertelsmann transformation index, country report: Kazakhstan. https://bti-project.org/content/en/downloads/reports/country_report_2014_KAZ.pdf

—. 2018. Bertelsmann transformation Index, country report: Kazakhstan. https://bti-project.org/content/en/downloads/reports/country_report_2018_KAZ.pdf

Bird R. 2019. Review of new World Bank framework "Innovations in Tax Compliance." ICTD Blog published 12 November 2019.

Booth, D. 2014. Aiding institutional reform in developing countries: Lessons from the Philippines on what works, what doesn't and why. ODI and The Asia Foundation.

Carraro, L., Rogers, J. and Rijicova, S. 2017. Technical support to improve design of targeted cash transfer program to be more responsive to the needs of families with children. Oxford: OPM.

Cbonds. 2019. Kazakhstan Bond Market. https://cbonds.com/country/Kazakhstan_bond/ Accessed in November 2019.

Chikanayev, S. 2012. Kazakhstan, The European Lawyer Reference Series: Project Finance Jurisdictional Comparisons. Nur-Sultan: GRATA International

Development Initiatives. 2015. Investments to End Poverty 2015.

Gabdullina, E. I. 2012. Evaluating the effectiveness of PPP projects as a mechanism for interaction between government and business in the region. In Modern problems of science and education. 2:3–8.

Government of Kazakhstan. 2015. Intended Nationally Determined Contribution - Submission of the Republic of Kazakhstan. Kazakhstan.

Hege, E. and Brimont, L. 2018. Integrating SDGs into national budgetary processes. IDDRI.

International Monetary Fund. 2017. Republic of Kazakhstan: Selected issues. IMF Country Report No 17/109. Washington, DC.

—. 2018. Republic of Kazakhstan: Selected issues. IMF Country Report No. 18/278. Washington, DC.

—. 2018a. Kazakhstan: 2018 article IV Consultation. IMF Country Report No. 18/277. Washington, DC.

—. 2018b. A Growth-Friendly Path for Building Fiscal Buffers in the Caucasus and Central Asia. Washington, DC.

—. 2019a. Kazakhstan: Staff concluding statement of an IMF staff visit. 17 July 2019.

—. 2019b. Regional Economic Outlook for Middle East and Central Asia. April. Washington, DC.

International Finance Corporation. 2017. Creating Markets in Kazakhstan: Country Private Sector Diagnostic. Washington, DC: World Bank.

International Tax Compact and Organisation for Economic Co-operation and Development. 2015. Examples of successful DRM reforms and the role of international co-operation, discussion paper. https://www.oecd.org/ctp/tax-global/examples-of-successful-DRM-reforms-and-the-role-of-international-co-operation.pdf

Organisation for Economic Co-operation and Development. 2008. Growing Unequal? Income Distribution and Poverty in OECD Countries. Paris: OECD Publishing.

—. 2012. Public Incentives and Performance System in Kazakhstan report. Paris: OECD Publishing.

—. 2014. Kazakhstan: Review of the Central Administration, OECD Public Governance Reviews. Paris: OECD Publishing.

—. 2016. Multi-dimensional review of Kazakhstan. OECD Development Pathways. Paris: OECD Publishing.

—. 2017. OECD Investment Policy Reviews: Kazakhstan. Paris: OECD Publishing..

—. 2018a. Country profiles: Institutional mechanisms for policy coherence, in Policy Coherence for Sustainable Development 2018: Towards Sustainable and Resilient Societies. Paris: OECD Publishing.

—. 2018b. SME and Entrepreneurship Policy in Kazakhstan 2018, OECD Studies on SMEs and Entrepreneurship. Paris: OECD Publishing.

—. 2019. Budgeting in Kazakhstan. OECD Journal on Budgeting: VOLUME 2018/3. Paris: OECD Publishing.

United Nations Development Programme. 2019a. Development Finance Assessment: Guidebook. https://www.asia-pacific.undp.org/content/rbap/en/home/library/sustainable-development/development-finance-assessment-guidebook.html

—. 2019b. Integrated Financing Solutions: How countries around the world are innovating to finance the sustainable development goals. https://www.asia-pacific.undp.org/content/rbap/en/home/library/sustainable-development/integrated-financing-solutions.html

UNECE. 2019. Kazakhstan environmental performance review. https://www.unece.org/environmental-policy/environmental-performance-reviews/enveprpublications/environmental-performance-reviews/2019/3rd-environmental-performance-review-of-kazakhstan/docs.html

United Nations. 2019. Inter-agency Task Force on Financing for Development. Financing for Sustainable Development Report. https://developmentfinance.un.org/

World Bank. 2016. High and Dry: Climate Change, Water, and the Economy. Washington, DC: World Bank.

—. 2017 Kazakhstan: Enhancing the Fiscal Framework to Support Economic Transformation. Public Finance Review. Washington, DC: World Bank.

—. 2018a. Consultation with the Government, Parliament, CSOs, NGOs, Think Tanks and Private.

—. 2018. Sector on the World Bank Group Country Partnership Framework for Kazakhstan FY19-23. Meeting Summary. 11–13 April.

—. 2018b. Kazakhstan systemic country diagnostic. Report no. 125611-kz. Washington, DC: World Bank.

—. 2018c. Public Expenditure and Financial Accountability Assessment. Washington, DC: World Bank.

—. 2018d. The State of Social Safety Nets. Washington, DC: World Bank.

—. 2019. World Development Indicators. Washington, DC: World Bank.

DATA APPENDIXES

Table 9. Overview table in % of Gross Domestic Product

Aggregate	Flow	2008	2009	2010	2011	2012	2013	2014	2015	2016	2017	2018
	Government revenue	**25,3%**	**20,2%**	**19,8%**	**19,5%**	**19,0%**	**17,7%**	**18,8%**	**18,3%**	**20,1%**	**21,6%**	**17,7%**
	Tax revenues	17,6%	13,1%	13,4%	14,1%	13,2%	13,3%	12,9%	11,9%	12,8%	12,5%	12,8%
	Non-tax revenues	0,5%	0,8%	0,5%	0,5%	0,9%	0,4%	0,5%	0,5%	0,8%	0,5%	0,4%
Domestic public finance	Proceeds from the sale of fixed capital	0,4%	0,2%	0,3%	0,2%	0,2%	0,2%	0,2%	0,2%	0,1%	0,1%	0,1%
	NFRK Transfers receipts	6,7%	6,5%	5,5%	4,2%	4,4%	3,9%	4,9%	6,0%	6,1%	8,1%	4,2%
	Other revenue	0,2%	-0,4%	0,1%	0,5%	0,3%	0,0%	0,3%	-0,4%	0,3%	0,3%	0,2%
	Domestic public debt	**0,1%**	**0,6%**	**1,0%**	**0,4%**	**0,4%**	**0,3%**	**1,4%**	**2,6%**	**1,8%**	**0,1%**	**0,8%**
Domestic commercial finance	**Commercial investment**	**10,6%**	**8,8%**	**8,7%**	**8,1%**	**9,4%**	**8,7%**	**9,4%**	**9,9%**	**9,7%**	**11,0%**	**13,2%**
	Domestic private debt	2,5%	3,4%	0,1%	4,8%	3,9%	4,0%	1,9%	1,5%	0,0%	0,2%	-0,1%
	Net ODA Received	**0,1%**	**0,1%**	**0,2%**	**0,0%**	**0,0%**	**0,0%**	**0,0%**	**0,0%**	**0,0%**	**0,0%**	**0,0%**
	ODA Grants	0,1%	0,1%	0,1%	0,0%	0,0%	0,0%	0,0%	0,0%	0,0%	0,0%	0,0%
International Public Finance	ODA Loans	0,0%	0,0%	0,0%	0,0%	0,0%	0,0%	0,0%	0,0%	0,0%	0,0%	0,0%
	ODA Equity investment	0,0%	0,0%	0,0%	0,0%	0,0%	0,0%	0,0%	0,0%	0,0%	0,0%	0,0%
	Other Official Flows	**0,0%**	**0,4%**	**1,2%**	**0,7%**	**0,5%**	**0,5%**	**0,7%**	**1,0%**	**1,4%**	**0,5%**	**0,0%**
	External public debt	**2,9%**	**4,2%**	**3,0%**	**2,4%**	**3,4%**	**2,7%**	**2,1%**	**1,0%**	**0,5%**	**3,2%**	**1,4%**
	Net Foreign Direct Investment	9,8%	8,7%	2,5%	4,5%	5,7%	3,4%	2,1%	1,8%	10,0%	2,3%	2,7%
	FDI Outflow	0,9%	2,7%	5,3%	2,8%	0,7%	1,0%	1,7%	0,4%	-3,8%	0,5%	-0,6%
	FDI Inflow	**10,7%**	**11,5%**	**7,8%**	**7,3%**	**6,4%**	**4,4%**	**3,8%**	**2,2%**	**6,2%**	**2,8%**	**2,1%**
	Net Portfolio investment	-7,0%	2,7%	5,7%	-6,7%	-8,4%	-2,5%	-0,5%	3,2%	-0,5%	3,2%	-1,5%
International private finance	Portfolio Outflows (Assets)	5,5%	-1,6%	4,9%	7,1%	7,2%	3,6%	2,9%	-5,2%	-0,9%	-1,9%	-0,6%
	Portfolio Inflows (Obligations)	-1,6%	1,1%	10,6%	0,4%	-1,1%	1,0%	2,5%	-2,0%	-1,5%	1,3%	-2,0%
	Net Remittances	0,0%	0,0%	0,0%	0,0%	0,0%	-0,4%	-0,4%	-0,5%	-0,3%	-0,4%	-0,4%
	Outward remittances (sent)	0,0%	0,0%	0,0%	0,0%	0,0%	0,7%	0,7%	0,8%	0,8%	0,9%	1,0%
	Inward Remittances	**0,1%**	**0,2%**	**0,2%**	**0,1%**	**0,1%**	**0,1%**	**0,2%**	**0,2%**	**0,3%**	**0,3%**	**0,3%**
	International commercial borrowing	**8,8%**	**8,5%**	**6,2%**	**3,0%**	**3,7%**	**5,2%**	**3,8%**	**-0,9%**	**8,6%**	**4,3%**	**0,7%**
	Revenue accruing to the NFRK*		**7,3%**	**5,5%**	**8,1%**	**7,9%**	**7,2%**	**8,6%**	**22,8%**	**0,0%**	**0,0%**	**5,1%**
	GRAND TOTAL	*57,2%*	*62,8%*	*64,2%*	*49,9%*	*49,8%*	*48,0%*	*51,2%*	*55,1%*	*47,2%*	*45,1%*	*39,3%*

FDI = foreign direct investment. NFRK = National fund of the Republic of Kazakhstan. ODA = official development assistance

Sources: MoF (government revenue and borrowing); MNE Statistics Committee (commercial investment). World Bank (remittances. international debt). Organisation for Economic Co-operation and Development (ODA. OOFs). National Bank of Kazakhstan (FDI and portfolio flows).

Overview table in T million, current

Aggregate	Flow	2008	2009	2010	2011	2012	2013	2014	2015	2016	2017	2018
	Government revenue	**4,064,078**	**3,442,604**	**4,323,929**	**5,508,396**	**5,906,539**	**6,383,344**	**7,454,001**	**7,466,402**	**9,451,554**	**11,718,888**	**10,939,393**
	Tax revenues	2,819,510	2,228,682	2,934,081	3,982,338	4,095,366	4,779,004	5,115,743	4,883,913	6,023,263	6,810,851	7,890,048
	Non-tax revenues	85,540	136,176	104,398	138,597	285,144	141,717	179,488	224,767	369,424	273,872	225,988
Domestic public finance	Proceeds from the sale of fixed capital	56,940	35,887	60,653	49,891	52,493	56,132	71,045	69,709	60,225	68,650	92,536
	NFRK Transfers receipts	1,072,421	1,104,600	1,200,000	1,200,000	1,380,000	1,405,500	1,955,000	2,456,417	2,855,574	4,414,317	2,600,000
	Other revenue	29,667	-62,741	24,797	137,570	93,536	991	132,725	-168,403	143,069	151,197	130,820
	Domestic public debt	**465,162**	**707,786**	**659,917**	**674,331**	**1,067,533**	**982,537**	**827,499**	**419,564**	**218,213**	**1,733,073**	**853,443**
	Commercial investment	**1,706,104**	**1,491,432**	**1,895,953**	**2,281,191**	**2,900,761**	**3,139,833**	**3,746,570**	**4,048,679**	**4,571,116**	**6,007,331**	**8,177,424**
Domestic commercial finance	Domestic private debt	395,972	579,719	23,008	1,351,572	1,203,793	1,423,630	746,282	606,005	12,706	131,634	-71,564
	Net ODA Received	**18,348**	**16,566**	**34,846**	**11,687**	**8,182**	**8,518**	**9,471**	**11,760**	**14,723**	**16,830**	**1,110**
	ODA Grants	18,020	16,046	24,166	11,474	7,969	8,518	9,471	11,760	14,723	16,830	1,110
International Public Finance	ODA Loans	–	–	10,680	–	–	–	–	–	–	–	–
	ODA Equity investment	328	520	–	212	213	–	–	–	–	–	–
	Other Official Flows	**7,793**	**61,101**	**262,128**	**200,834**	**159,901**	**172,049**	**263,174**	**423,756**	**680,808**	**257,203**	**–**
	External public debt	**12,135**	**101,645**	**222,312**	**105,579**	**111,373**	**120,610**	**538,846**	**1,059,878**	**836,380**	**71,996**	**493,660**
	Net Foreign Direct Investment	1,577,704	1,487,287	540,073	1,258,387	1,767,826	1,222,270	837,636	723,161	4,703,462	1,224,498	1,674,452
	FDI Outflow	145,204	465,982	1,161,925	790,344	220,854	347,864	683,579	176,312	-1,791,171	297,699	-380,130
	FDI Inflow	**1,722,907**	**1,953,269**	**1,701,998**	**2,048,731**	**1,988,680**	**1,570,134**	**1,521,215**	**899,473**	**2,912,291**	**1,522,197**	**1,294,322**
	Net Portfolio investment	-1,128,115	456,225	1,248,094	-1,886,728	-2,592,709	-917,898	-186,151	1,305,518	-255,321	1,759,858	-907,580
International private finance	Portfolio Outflows (Assets)	875,500	-275,641	1,061,229	1,992,606	2,246,821	1,293,563	1,160,037	-2,111,870	-427,767	-1,058,502	-343,908
	Portfolio Inflows (Obligations)	-252,615	180,584	2,309,323	105,878	-345,888	375,666	973,886	-806,352	-683,088	701,356	-1,251,488
	Net Remittances	–	–	–	–	–	-148,301	-156,987	-206,212	-133,656	-190,467	-239,850
	Outward remittances (sent)	–	–	–	–	–	238,821	275,937	334,986	382,173	496,578	601,816
	Inward Remittances	**15,106**	**29,235**	**33,236**	**26,349**	**42,196**	**51,938**	**71,923**	**65,248**	**131,446**	**182,697**	**213,044**
	International commercial borrowing	**1,416,650**	**1,453,213**	**1,351,374**	**839,862**	**1,153,768**	**1,885,795**	**1,501,655**	**-381,484**	**4,036,136**	**2,329,331**	**407,368**
	Revenue accruing to the NFRK*		1,234,900	1,207,723	2,288,044	2,463,885	2,586,104	3,411,851	9,337,214			3,155,588
	GRAND TOTAL	**9,175,669**	**10,672,335**	**14,002,740**	**14,090,880**	**15,456,929**	**17,276,528**	**20,320,091**	**22,544,138**	**22,169,580**	**24,540,902**	**24,283,864**

FDI = foreign direct investment, NFRK = National fund of the Republic of Kazakhstan, ODA = official development assistance

Sources: MoF (government revenue and borrowing); MNE Statistics Committee (commercial investment), World Bank (remittances, international debt), Organisation for Economic Co-operation and Development (ODA, OOFs), National Bank of Kazakhstan (FDI and portfolio flows).

Overview table in $ million, current

Aggregate	Flow	2008	2009	2010	2011	2012	2013	2014	2015	2016	2017	2018
	Government revenue											
	Tax revenues	33,783	23,340	29,345	37,569	39,612	41,960	41,598	33,673	27,623	35,948	31,735
	Non-tax revenues	23,437	15,110	19,912	27,161	27,465	31,414	28,549	22,026	17,604	20,892	22,889
Domestic public finance	Proceeds from the sale of fixed capital	711	923	709	945	1,912	932	1,002	1,014	1,080	840	656
	NFRK Transfers receipts	473	243	412	340	352	369	396	314	176	211	268
	Other revenue	8,915	7,489	8,144	8,184	9,255	9,239	10,910	11,078	8,346	13,541	7,543
	Domestic public debt	247	-425	168	938	627	7	741	-759	418	464	380
Domestic commercial finance	**Commercial investment**	3,867	4,799	4,479	4,599	7,159	6,459	4,618	1,892	638	5,316	2,476
	Domestic private debt	14,182	10,111	12,867	15,559	19,454	20,639	20,908	18,259	13,360	18,427	23,723
	Net ODA Received	3,292	3,930	156	9,218	8,073	9,358	4,165	2,733	37	404	-208
	ODA Grants	153	112	236	80	55	56	53	53	43	52	3
International Public Finance	ODA Loans	150	109	164	78	53	56	53	53	43	52	3
	ODA Equity investment	-	-	72	-	-	-	-	-	-	-	-
	Other Official Flows	3	4	-	1	1	-	-	-	-	-	-
	External public debt	65	414	1,779	1,370	1,072	1,131	1,469	1,911	1,990	789	-
	Net Foreign Direct Investment	101	689	1,509	720	747	793	3,007	4,780	2,444	221	1,432
	FDI Outflow	13,115	10,083	3,665	8,583	11,856	8,034	4,675	3,261	13,746	3,756	4,858
	FDI Inflow	1,207	3,159	7,885	5,390	1,481	2,287	3,815	795	-5,235	913	-1,103
	Net Portfolio investment	14,322	13,243	11,551	13,973	13,337	10,321	8,489	4,057	8,511	4,669	3,755
International private finance	Portfolio Outflows (Assets)	-9,378	3,093	8,470	-12,868	-17,388	-6,034	-1,039	5,888	-746	5,398	-2,633
	Portfolio Inflows (Obligations)	7,278	-1,869	7,202	13,590	15,068	8,503	6,474	-9,525	-1,250	-3,247	-998
	Net Remittances	-2,100	1,224	15,672	722	-2,320	2,469	5,435	-3,637	-1,996	2,151	-3,631
	Outward remittances (sent)	-	-	-	-	-	-975	-876	-930	-391	-584	-696
	Inward Remittances	-	-	-	-	-	1,570	1,540	1,511	1,117	1,523	1,746
	International commercial borrowing	126	198	226	180	283	341	401	294	384	560	618
	Revenue accruing to the NFRK*	11,776	9,852	9,171	5,728	7,738	12,396	8,380	-1,720	11,796	7,145	1,182
			8,372	8,196	15,605	16,524	16,999	19,040	42,111			9,154
	GRAND TOTAL	79,565	76,285	95,187	105,323	111,734	122,922	117,564	104,407	64,830	75,683	70,240

FDI = foreign direct investment, NFRK = National fund of the Republic of Kazakhstan, ODA = official development assistance

Sources: MoF (government revenue and borrowing); MNE Statistics Committee (commercial investment), World Bank (remittances, international debt), Organisation for Economic Co-operation and Development (ODA, OOFs), National Bank of Kazakhstan (FDI and portfolio flows).

www.ingramcontent.com/pod-product-compliance
Lightning Source LLC
Chambersburg PA
CBHW050050220326
41599CB00045B/7361